# Losing America's Schools

# Losing America's Schools

## *The Fight to Reclaim Public Education*

Nancy E. Bailey

ROWMAN & LITTLEFIELD
Lanham • Boulder • New York • London

Published by Rowman & Littlefield
A wholly owned subsidiary of The Rowman & Littlefield Publishing Group, Inc.
4501 Forbes Boulevard, Suite 200, Lanham, Maryland 20706
www.rowman.com

Unit A, Whitacre Mews, 26-34 Stannary Street, London SE11 4AB



British Library Cataloguing in Publication Information Available

**Library of Congress Cataloging-in-Publication Data Available**

ISBN 978-1-4758-2861-0 (cloth : alk. paper)
ISBN 978-1-4758-2862-7 (pbk. : alk. paper)
ISBN 978-1-4758-2863-4 (Electronic)

∞™ The paper used in this publication meets the minimum requirements of American National Standard for Information Sciences Permanence of Paper for Printed Library Materials, ANSI/NISO Z39.48-1992.

Printed in the United States of America

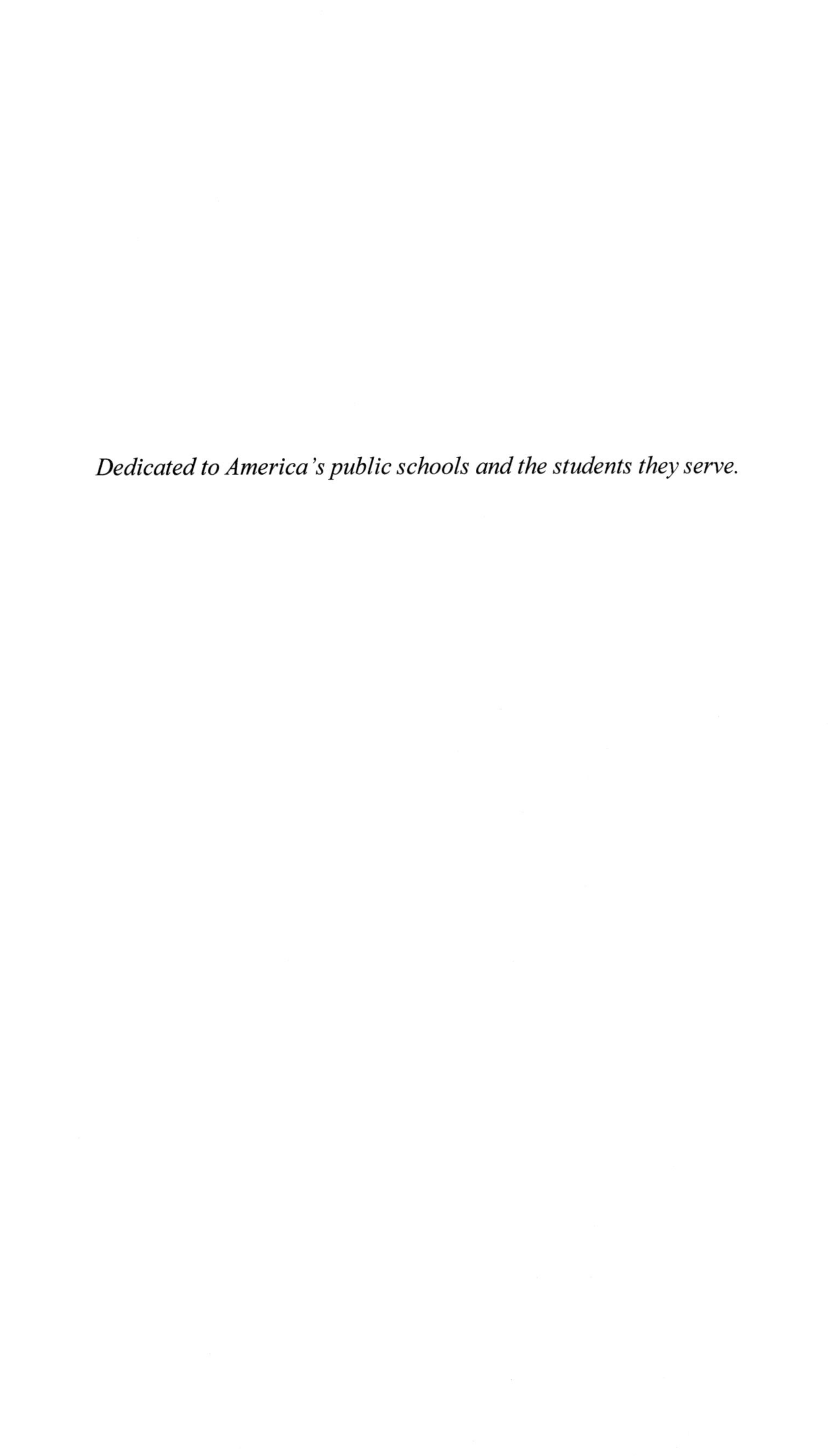

*Dedicated to America's public schools and the students they serve.*

# Contents

# Preface

It is difficult to write about loss. That is why writing about how Americans are losing their democratic public schools has not been easy. But having been a longtime educator and recognizing the benefits of public schools, and believing strongly in the worth of every child, I forged forward.

Struggling against the corporate world of public school privatization has become a battle. The stakes are high. I know that despite whatever words I write, the life of our public schools might remain in jeopardy. We now face a serious risk that we will lose the free, quality public education to which we were once accustomed.

As Americans, we will no longer be able to claim public schools as our own. With unregulated charter schools, we might even lose a well-educated populace. But our education system is worth fighting for, and I see this struggle taking place across the country. Parents and teachers are reclaiming *their* public schools. They recognize that a democratic public school system reflects who we are as a people.

I grew up attending public schools and taught in public schools. I find public schools remarkable places, because no matter where you come from or who you are, no matter your religious beliefs, or disabilities, everyone is welcome. Good public schools bring children from all backgrounds together, creating rich diversity and helping us all build tolerance for one another. Good public schools shore up the weaknesses in children and highlight the strengths of students and what they can become. Public schools are a key part of the foundation of the United States of America.

Public schools have never been perfect. When public schools have failed, however, it has often been due to lacking resources, poverty, and mismanagement. In general, public schools must constantly evolve—always improve. But those changes should benefit children—not disgrace them. Reform should lift students, not cast them as failures.

I previously wrote about troubling reforms affecting the schools and programs for children in *Misguided Education Reform: Debating the Impact on Students*. This book, *Losing America's Schools: The Fight to Reclaim Public Education*, is more about the structure of those reforms and how they have taken root. Both books argue for good, supportive public schools for all children.

America has for too long permitted the wealthier among us to privatize public schools, taking charge of them and stealing what rightfully belongs to the public—to all of us. Our public schools served us well in the past. They can serve us well again.

# Acknowledgments

I wish to thank my husband, Charles Bailey, for his patience and support while I wrote this book. I would also like to thank Sheila Resseger, Doug Martin, and Roger Titcombe—strong voices for children in their own right—for their professional reviews. And last, thank you to my editor at Rowman & Littlefield, Tom Koerner, for his support in this endeavor.

# Introduction

> There's a campaign under way to essentially destroy the public education system, the system which is based on the principle that you care if some other child who you don't know gets an education. That's the public education system. There's an attempt to destroy that, along with every aspect of human life and attitudes and thought that involve social solidarity. It's being done in all sorts of ways. One is simply by underfunding. So if you make the public schools really rotten, people will look for an alternative.
>
> —Noam Chomsky[1]

The purpose of this book is to look at six factors that have been instrumental in the destruction of public schooling: the corporate takeover, charter schools, jobs and the economy, religion, the deprofessionalization of educators, and an overemphasis on technology. These changes have put our democratic public school system in danger.

But the American people increasingly are struggling to stop the harmful reforms tied to those issues—to stop the privatization of public schools. This book looks at how America found itself on the path to systematically destroying its democratic public schools, and what we are doing now to stop it.

*Losing America's Schools: The Fight to Reclaim Public Education* is a sequel and companion to my first book, *Misguided Education Reform: Debating the Impact on Students*. In that book, the focus was on the problems of reform in the areas of early childhood, testing, reading, special education, excessive use of discipline, the loss of the arts, and the problem of substandard school facilities. This new book covers the structural problems of school reform.

Chapter 1 describes how the past thirty years since *A Nation at Risk* have seen an unjustifiable attack on public schools by corporate America. I note economist Milton Friedman's ideology of school privatization. Every president since Ronald Reagan has worked, along with CEOs and think tanks, to transform public schools into a business model. It has not worked. It has left us with segregated, harshly run, dreary schools that squander tax dollars. Corporate CEOs, politicians, and entrepreneurs all drive school reform, though most have never worked in schools. They know little about the students whose lives they affect.

Chapter 2 explains how public schools have arbitrarily been converted into unproven charter schools in major cities. In places such as New Orleans, there are few real public schools left. Children born into poverty attend these schools in the midst of a strictly run environment that often disregards their true abilities.

Charter schools create a dueling educational system, stealing tax dollars from the real public schools they are designed to replace. Most charters run with little transparency, and they separate and ignore students with disabilities and language differences. Despite unproven charter school effectiveness, real public schools continue to close due to high-stakes testing and arbitrary accountability measures.

Chapter 3 explores the claims that students are unable to compete economically with other countries because of insufficient schooling. What is behind the negative talk about public schools and the economy, and how did standards become a part of this conversation? Why are all students pushed to go to college? What is the job outlook? What futures do students now face when it comes to employment?

By using the deceptive excuse of a poor economy, corporations have been able to commandeer the message of "education for all" to "education for a chosen few." Many students graduate college facing troubling job prospects. Public schools are unfairly described as "dropout factories," and students often are steered into careers without regard for their interests and needs. This chapter will explore the connections between school and work.

Chapter 4 discusses the increasing involvement of religion with public schooling. It explores separation of church and state, charter schools, and school vouchers. Those who argue for choice fail to hold private and parochial schools accountable, and religion is often entangled in the choice debate. Charter schools run with little, if any, oversight, and they have never proven themselves to be better than traditional public schools.

Chapter 5 investigates the deprofessionalization of educators—looking at teachers, principals, superintendents, and other school leaders. What kind of preparation is expected of such professionals? Replacing educators with those who know little about children, in roles traditionally designed for real educators, leaves us vulnerable. It has also been personally destructive in the lives of children and their families.

The teaching profession has been vilified to fulfill the for-profit privatization dream of the late economist Milton Friedman. I examine the troubling support given programs designed to replace traditional education programs, including Teach for America, The New Teacher Project, New Leaders, and the Broad Superintendent Academy. I also discuss the Relay Graduate School of Education.

Chapter 6 deals with the overinflated and unjustifiable belief that technology can replace brick-and-mortar schools. This has led to a harmful restructuring of learning that affects the schooling of our youngest students. Thus far, there is no proof that virtual schools are better than public schooling. I investigate programs such as the for-profit online company K12 Inc. and the controversial Rocketship charter schools. Competency-Based Education is also discussed.

Hidden behind the glitz of the education reform movement is a groundswell of parents, teachers, education administrators, politicians, citizens, and students who are tired of the draconian changes they see happening to their public schools. While outsiders have been given unbridled control over many facets of schooling, more educators and parents are speaking out at school board meetings and taking back control of their schools.

Many parents once embraced charter schools, but that, too, is changing. More parents and teachers are speaking out against charters and on behalf of real public schools. They do not like corporations seizing the power of school boards and making decisions about public schooling that should belong to them.

Contrary to what many school reformers would like the public to believe, many Americans support their public schools and teachers. They want their voices heard. *Losing America's Schools: The Fight to Reclaim Public Education* is a book about this struggle. Both this book and *Misguided Education Reform: Debating the Impact on Students* attempt to bring us back to democratic public schools that open doors to all children. Both books highlight the kind of public schools children in America deserve.

## NOTE

1. David Barsamian and Noam Chomsky, *Propaganda and the Public Mind: Conversations with Noam Chomsky* (Chicago: Haymarket Books, 2001), 113.

# *Chapter One*

# Corporate Takeover

> Our nation is at risk. Our once unchallenged preeminence in commerce, industry, science and technological innovation is being overtaken by competitors throughout the world.
>
> —*A Nation at Risk*[1]

## SCHOOL PRIVATIZATION

Public school privatization gained momentum during the Reagan administration with the idea that parents should be able to choose the schools they wanted for their children through tax credit in the form of vouchers. At the time, most parents were satisfied with their local public schools. But eventually, with the nonstop negative drone of the mainstream media, aided by businessmen and politicians on both sides of the aisle, Americans came to believe that their public schools and teachers had failed.

Public schools had problems, especially in inner cities and some poor rural areas, but they had never failed as badly as Americans were led to believe. The Reagan ultraconservatives, including a chosen panel called the National Commission on Excellence in Education in 1983, devised the blue-ribbon report, *A Nation at Risk: The Imperative for Educational Reform*. The report painted an ominous picture of public schools. One statement suggested America's education programs were "eroded by a rising tide of mediocrity that threatens our very future as a Nation and a people."[2]

Much has been written about *A Nation at Risk*, and it is still spoken about today. Despite glaring inconsistencies and lacking validation, it succeeded at its primary purpose—to stir up fear and distrust about school quality and the nation's ability to compete with other countries. It heralded the message that government-run public schools missed the mark and that something dramatic needed to change. With the wheels set in motion, the United States began its condemnation of public schools.

One of the means of attack included severe budget cuts. These cuts were illustrated well in President Reagan's own high school, a public school, in Dixon, Illinois. The school had been a shining success story, but in 1985, Dixon faced the loss of revered, long-standing programs, including the football team Reagan once played on and the marching band that performed at his inauguration (Kleinknecht, 2009, 6). The president, despite a friend's pleading, refused to come to the aid of the school.

While the president rejected the idea of providing federal assistance to his alma mater, he expressed delight when the Dixon Kiwanis Club gave funds to save the school's newspaper—clearly demonstrating the new mindset that private partnership is better than public funding. The donation from the Kiwanis Club, however, could not save the school, and voters had to eventually pass a property tax increase to salvage the other programs. Dixon High School, like many public schools across the country, would never fully recover.

Many politicians, including President Reagan, embraced economist Milton Friedman's free market business ideology. Friedman, an economic advisor to the president, started writing about school choice in 1955. He believed in competition and vouchers for parents. He condemned the nineteenth-century industrial model of education and derided public school districts as monopolies.

Friedman's influence is still felt in many facets of American life—including the push to privatize public schools. His organization, the Friedman Foundation for Educational Choice, is still active today, despite his death in 2006. Milton Friedman's influence—most notably in New Orleans after Katrina—will be discussed more in chapter 2.

As President Reagan continued his rally against government-run programs and taxes, he attempted to eliminate the Department of Education started under President Jimmy Carter. At the same time, desegregation rulings from *Brown v. the Board of Education* had resulted in societal turmoil surrounding changes to cities and student populations found in urban schools.

While suburban sprawl and poverty in the inner cities were tough issues to tackle, the Reagan administration had started a domino effect with every president who followed—the ultimate goal to privatize public schools. Many in the business community and various religious leaders were on board for the change.

## NEW AMERICAN SCHOOLS

> America 2000 identifies some aspects of schooling that need attention, but these are clouded by questionable policies, inadequate funding, and a tendency to talk the game of localism while pursuing a strategy of federalism from the top. The entire proposal lacks a sense of reality about the situation of children and youth in America. Their growing diversity is ignored, their growing poverty is not even mentioned, and muddled thinking about their motivation suggests that forcing them to fail tests will awaken their desire to learn.
>
> —Harold Howe II, former Commissioner of Education[3]

Newly elected President George H. W. Bush talked about being the "education president," but there was little action, at first, on the part of his administration, to do much about education. Then, in 1989, the president called together the nation's governors in an unprecedented education summit in Charlottesville, Virginia. The meeting echoed *A Nation at Risk* and continued to promote public schools in crisis. National standards, frowned upon under President Reagan, were highlighted at the meeting. Almost every governor had a list of items that they believed schools were lacking and needed to do to improve, but President Bush's federal spending plan was sparse.

Seven hundred journalists and the major television stations lent an air of urgency to the occasion (Goodgame, 1989). The four key proposals to come out of the summit were school choice involving magnet schools and district open enrollment, easing teacher licensing requirements, partnerships with business, and test requirements for graduation and promotion. Then Governor Clinton was described as one of the "key players" at the meeting.[4]

By the late 1980s and early 1990s, public school educators began to notice business becoming more involved in schools. Corporate employees started taking time to tutor students at public schools under the teacher's direction. These business/school partnerships seemed an appropriate way for businesses to help students. But more changes and posturing were taking place behind the scenes.

President Bush, like his predecessor, supported vouchers and choice. *The Nation* chronicled how Bush, in 1991, along with US Education secretary Lamar Alexander and "a roomful of Fortune 500 CEOs" (teachers were not included), started a private nonprofit as part of America 2000 called the New American Schools Development Corporation (NASDC). Its purpose was to usher in "corporate America" as the "savior of the nation's schoolchildren," the message that public schools had failed, and the promise to create "a new generation of American Schools."[5] The NASDC, with a Democratic Congress, never generated enough funding for continuing reform projects but called for standards, business executive CEOs as school leaders, charter schools, and noncredentialed teachers.

The same report describes how teachers were disregarded as professionals—described as "conduits and cops, carrying information and enforcing rules"—and children were treated as "little more than receptacles, whose ability to contain the prescribed information can best be measured in an objective national knowledge test."[6] While these ideas did not hold much weight for school reform at the time, they eventually became more prevalent and the basis for school reform.

The NASDC ignored decades of child education research, and instead relied on proposals from William Bennett, Dennis Doyle, and Chester Finn Jr., noneducators who can still be found pushing today's public school reform. Bennett would go on to become one of the owners of the for-profit K12 Inc., a virtual school program with a trail of poor results, heavily funded by tax dollars.

The online program is used in school districts, charter schools, and homeschools around the country despite serious concerns about its effectiveness. In 2015, now state senator Lamar Alexander (R-Tenn.) became one of the coarchitects of the Every Student Achieves Act to replace No Child Left Behind. Many fear the bill is a giveaway to charter schools.

America 2000 focused on the creation of national standards and voluntary tests in fourth, eighth, and twelfth grade. It emphasized five core subjects—English, math, science, history, and geography—and proposed setting up schools that would be models for other schools. Schools and school districts would get a report card (US Department of Education, States Impact on Federal Education Policy).

David Kearns, the deputy secretary of education who had been CEO of IBM, visited towns to push the idea of America 2000 communities. The educational goals he emphasized included school readiness, high graduation rates, world-class math and science, adult literacy, and drug- and violence-free schools (O'Brien, 1992).

The New American Schools (NAS) became the group's new title. Many groups formed with similar objectives to forward privatization, and although the title changed, the objectives started with NAS are alive and creating controversy in education still today.

## EDISON SCHOOLS

School reformers rarely acknowledge that folksy, bow-tied businessman and dabbler in entrepreneurial ventures, Chris Whittle, unsuccessfully attempted to make for-profit schools starting in 1991, but they did not work. The *Esquire* magazine publisher began his foray into the school business with Channel One news, a program for high school students which is still in existence, and even more recently advertising the hotly debated Common Core State Standards. Channel One originally generated controversy due to its advertisement—a deluge of junk food and military ads. Whittle no longer owns the program.

Around this time, schools also began to heavily advertise corporate products under the pretense that business leaders were getting involved and helping schools. Sodas and snacks became readily available in schools for a fee. Discount tickets to stores and restaurants flooded schools for student and teacher rewards.

Whittle promised Americans that Edison schools, run by tax dollars, would be better than public schools, and that they would make a profit. The schools were backed by free market ideologues, including:

- Tom Ingram, Tennessee campaign manager and chief of staff to former Tennessee governor and education secretary Lamar Alexander (1991–1993), who went on to be a lead negotiator on the revision of No Child Left Behind, resulting in the Every Student Succeeds Act.
- Benno C. Schmidt Jr., past Yale president who is also the chairman of Whittle's current school, Avenues: The World School, in New York City.
- Edison's chief education officer, the late John Chubb. Chubb, a political scientist from the Hoover and Brookings Institute, with Terry Moe, who is the William Bennett Munro Professor of Political Science at Stanford, penned the book promoting school choice titled *Politics, Markets, and America's Schools*.
- Founding Edison partner and senior scholar Chester Finn Jr. He is currently the distinguished senior fellow and president emeritus at the Thomas B.

Fordham Institute and senior fellow at Stanford's Hoover Institution. He continues to work on school reform.
- Richard Barth, CEO of the KIPP Foundation (charter schools), married to Wendy Kopp, founder of Teach for America. He served as Edison School's president of District Partnership.

Edison Schools, along with forty-seven other educational management organizations, operated with the promise to do better than public schools. But Edison had unresolved problems and ran with little oversight. To save money, they used services provided by the local school district while competing against them. Student disciplinary problems festered after Edison dismissed experienced special education teachers to train their own (Moberg, 2004). Difficult students were pushed out of the schools.

In *The Edison Schools: Corporate Schooling and the Assault on Public Education*, Kenneth Saltman described Edison School problems in detail. He notes: "Walking through an Edison school, one is struck by how similar it looks to any other public or even private school. Initially, however, Edison schools were not supposed to look like other schools."[7]

In addition, Whittle sought to run public schools to make a profit. Money went to upper management instead of student instruction. Curriculum changes involved longer days, repetitive testing, and using computers. Students showed little improvement.

By 2003, Edison School popularity nosedived along with the school stock. In a strange twist, Florida's teacher pension funds were used to bail Whittle and failed Edison out of their slump. Edison Schools, the largest publically traded school, which never turned a profit, received a $182 million buyout by the State of Florida (Caputo, 2003).

With help from the teachers, criticized as failures by those favoring for-profit schools, Whittle repackaged himself. He started several charter schools and EdisonLearning, a nonprofit that sells online programs, including Magic Johnson Bridgescape, e-courses, and school management advice to the United States and the United Kingdom (EdisonLearning). It also includes Provost Academy, an online charter school.

In 2012, Whittle's new *private* school opened in New York. Avenues: The World School covers nursery through high school. Investors backed the school with $75 million, and parents currently pay $45,350 a year for admission. Twenty more Avenue schools are planned for around the world, and Edison School promoters are still found in powerful school venues, working to privatize public schools. Whittle resigned from the Avenues in 2015 and sits on the board of the Center for Education Reform.

## THE SANDIA REPORT

The Sandia Report is rarely mentioned when discussing public schools; however, if its findings had been publicized Americans might have looked at public schools and teachers differently. One of the best descriptions of what happened with the Sandia Report was published in a book that is just as relevant to education and public schools today as when it first appeared in 1995.

In *The Manufactured Crisis: Myths, Fraud, and the Attack on America's Public Schools*, authors David C. Berliner and Bruce J. Biddle describe the Sandia Report as probably a "tragic mistake" by the President George H. W. Bush administration.[8] At that time, Admiral James Watkins asked Sandia National Libraries, a part of the Department of Energy in New Mexico, to complete a study about the condition of America's public schools. They likely had convinced themselves that the results would provide added proof that public schools were failing.

The Sandia researchers, having done research on higher education, were commissioned to conduct a local, state, and national analysis of schools. What they found contradicted many of the bad things being said about public schools during the Reagan and Bush administrations. Robert M. Huelskamp, who worked on the Sandia Report, in 1993 explained the findings in a *Phi Delta Kappan* article summarized below.

Highlighting the results: the Sandia researchers found "steady or slightly improving trends."[9] Graduation rates had remained steady, somewhere between 75 percent and 80 percent, for more than twenty years. America had the best graduation rate in the world!

While some students took longer to finish high school, others completed their General Education Development (GED) test. Public schools in the inner cities needed to improve—urban youth dropped out too frequently and minority students continued to lag behind their white peers on standardized tests. But they *also performed better* on the tests than they did fifteen years earlier. Black, Hispanic, and Native American students trailed their white peer group's scores by one hundred points. But there was *no* overall drastic performance decline.

Almost 60 percent of students attended accredited institutions, and two-thirds enrolled in four-year institutions. Despite fears surrounding science, 200,000 students earned bachelor's degrees in the natural sciences and engineering every year. Female and minority students at that time, however, received fewer technical degrees.

Education spending rose in part due to special education. Insurance and retirement funds also caused a large part of the cost hikes. Compared to other countries, though, education spending appeared average. America never overspent on education when matched to their outside counterparts.

The Sandia Report's information concerning international test comparisons indicated that even though the United States lagged behind other countries in special areas, the technical degree attainment was one of the best in the world. Scientists also noted the difficulty in obtaining credible data due to differences between the educational systems of different countries. Not all schools run alike.

But student performance on the National Assessment of Educational Progress (NAEP) indicated steady or improving performance for the United States. The reason SAT scores declined was because *more* students from the bottom half of the class took the test. Known as "Simpson's paradox," the testing changes had to do with including groups that had been excluded in the past. Overall scores looked worse than they were due to combining the groups. If students from the top quartile had been the only ones continuing to take the test, the scores would have been high—like earlier years.

In regard to teachers, the Sandia Report describes how, through teacher interviews, it was discovered that public school problems were often blamed on teachers, resulting in their low self-esteem, and that *this* threatened the quality of future schooling. The researchers considered this a serious issue. Yet ignoring this information has led to an increasingly destructive decline of teacher professionalism in America.

Workplace skills for students after graduation were *not* found to be wanting. Company training had more to do with punctuality and how to dress well, and it often involved immigrants, not recent graduates, as Americans were led to believe. In other words, America's students were doing well in many facets of education. Only Germany and Japan provided more job training than the United States.

There were difficulties with the changing demographics of students. Immigration had increased in this country in the 1980s, and Sandia researchers saw the influx of the children of immigrants into public schools as a concern, partly due to changes that included 150 different languages. Family dynamics were seen to be shifting due to more single-parent homes and homes where both parents worked. These societal modifications heavily impacted how schools would meet student needs.

The Sandia Report raised concerns about the widespread message that reform required new, untested programs, and this came with little understanding of future outcomes. Recommendations emphasized having local, state, and federal governments work together to improve schools. All of this would require strong leadership and finding better ways to address the needs of minority and urban students. Special attention would be needed to address the changes involving immigrants and demographics. The report mentioned upgrading the quality of available data regarding education.

Daniel Tanner, a professor at Rutgers University, originally provided much of the research concerning the Sandia Report. As the Clinton administration prepared to take over in 2000, Tanner wrote another article published in *Phi Delta Kappan* alerting educators of things to come:

> With a new Administration in Washington, one might be tempted to conclude that the prescriptions in America 2000, President Bush's strategy for school reform, will no longer be taken seriously and will not be implemented. However, we must remember that America 2000 grew out of a meeting of the nation's governors and that, while President Bush convened the meeting, Bill Clinton—then governor of Arkansas—played a key role in defining the national education goals for the year 2000. Although this does not place President Clinton in the same camp as his predecessor, we are at a critical turning point with regard to the federal role in public education, and some key reform proposals in America 2000 have been endorsed by the Clinton Administration, under the rubric of Goals 2000.
>
> These proposals need to be questioned—and in some cases challenged—by our profession in view of the powerful and readily available contravening sources of evidence. Indeed, we need to examine them in light of a national study of education that was effectively suppressed by the Bush Administration when the data contradicted most of the allegations, premises, and proposals on which America 2000 was based. Such suppression of information on virtually any national concern other than education would make sensational copy for the media. However school-bashing makes better copy than a report revealing that the public schools are performing reasonably well and, indeed, as well as they ever have.[10]

While the Sandia Report was published in the *Journal of Educational Research*, it never got the huge press of *A Nation at Risk.* Available only to a few scholars, today it is mostly forgotten. We will never know what the impact of the Sandia Report would have been if the findings had been taken more seriously.

However, it would appear to be significant to revisit history and discuss what had gone right in public schools at that juncture in time. What debates should have taken place? The Sandia Report could still provide us with a better understanding of the problems then and a different outlook concerning the evaluation of public schools today.

## THE BUSINESS ROUNDTABLE

> I accept your premise; we can only do better with tougher standards and better assessment, and you should set the standards. I believe that is absolutely right. And that will be the lasting legacy of this conference. I also believe, along with Mr. Gerstner and the others who are here, that it's very important not only for businesses to speak out for reform, but for business leaders to be knowledgeable enough to know what reform to speak out for, and what to emphasize, and how to hammer home the case for higher standards, as well as how to help local school districts change some of the things that they are now doing so that they have a reasonable chance at meeting these standards.
>
> —President Bill Clinton [11]

In *Why Is Corporate America Bashing Our Public Schools?* Kathy Emery and Susan Ohanian describe how Arkansas governor Bill Clinton, along with President H. W. Bush and IBM's CEO Lou Gerstner, originally met with the Business Roundtable to craft a plan for public schools (2004, 141–64). According to the authors, much of the agenda came from the California Business Roundtable (CBR) report *Restructuring California Education: A Design for Public Education in the Twenty-First Century.* Goals 2000 emphasized standardized testing, core competencies, and standards.

Gerstner's ideas for drastic changes to schools appeared in a book he coauthored with Roger D. Semerad and Denis Philip Doyle, titled *Reinventing Education: Entrepreneurship in America's Public Schools* (1995), heralding the question: Can IBM reinvent schools? The book is filled with market-driven tactics for school reform. We still hear the cry for more homework, a longer day, and a longer school year—all questionable reforms. Other parts of the book display plans still playing out involving privatization and technology.

Gerstner complained that schools were not changing—that they were old-fashioned—and he insisted students were not doing as well historically. His whole premise involved impressing upon the American people that students performed worse than their counterparts in other countries. The real problems, he emphasized, were in math and science (4–5). Today, we hear the same concerns about science, technology, engineering, and math, otherwise known as STEM. Yet in reality, it can be argued that no such critical problems really existed then, or now.

By 2002, *The Nation* noted how language changes relating to public schools had become noticeably geared toward business: "Gerstner describes schoolchildren as human capital, teachers as sellers in a marketplace and the public school system as a monopoly. Predictably, CEOs brought to education reform CEO rhetoric: stringent, intolerant of failure, even punitive—hence the word 'sanction,' as if some schools had been turning away weapons inspectors."[12] Words such as *lockdown* and *zero tolerance* displayed a sense of coldness regarding children and changed the way the public viewed schools and school climate.[13]

Goals 2000 made way for the Bush administration's No Child Left Behind (NCLB), and corporate lobbyists increasingly influenced how schools would be run. High-stakes testing was used to close schools and condemn teachers. School board decisions, instead of reflecting the voice of constituents, began to reflect a business ideology. More communities embraced the ideas first endorsed by *A Nation at Risk* and America 2000. Privatization supporters who sought to find a way to discredit public schools in the eyes of parents made great gains. Democrats united with Republicans concerning NCLB.

The Obama administration brought new hope that refreshing changes were in order for public schools, but President Obama and US Education Secretary Arne Duncan would carry on the principles of NCLB with even harsher consequences. While they provided states a way out of NCLB with waivers, Race to the Top (RTTT) became the president's $4.35 billion signature effort to push reform forward. States were rewarded by a continuance of the draconian educational policies involving testing and performance-based standards.

The Obama administration also insisted states lift caps on the number of charter schools that could be created. Schools collected more testing data on children. Instead of child-friendly programs, many public schools continued to close due to arbitrary claims that they were not performing. Teachers were replaced with recruits from Teach for America. Many of the shuttered schools had been underfunded for years.

All of this paved the way for Common Core State Standards as parents increasingly came to believe that their public schools failed. For years, parents approved of *their* public schools, convinced that other schools failed. Even in the 2012 Phi Delta Kappan, PDK/Gallup polls, parents liked their schools (Lopez, 2011). But as they listened to the media's negative reporting, critical of public schools and teachers, and as time passed and budget cuts to schools increased, the American public became increasingly convinced that public schools are failed institutions.

## VENTURE PHILANTHROPY

> Venture capitalists of Silicon Valley, who have backed hundreds of high-technology entrepreneurs, are eagerly financing a new group these days: schoolmasters.
>
> —James Flanigan, *New York Times*[14]

In 1998, the NewSchools Venture Fund (NSVF) began to radically transform public education by helping to support entrepreneur-driven reforms. Since that time, they have raised more than $250 million for this effort. NSVF funnels money into a range of charter school companies, and these companies also receive government funding originally destined for traditional public schools.

Many who have worked with NSVF have gone on to important appointments in the US Department of Education. Joanne Weiss, chief operating officer at the NSVF, was also Secretary of Education Arne Duncan's chief of staff. Weiss has a degree in biochemistry but no experience working with children as a teacher and no education degree. She had an active role in President Obama's Race to the Top initiatives.

Nonprofit charter schools are like for-profit charter schools in that they collect tax dollars that would have ordinarily gone to the common good of public schools. In a nonprofit organization, the operators still can earn fat salaries and funnel funds to outside for-profit organizations.

When governors and legislators cut school budgets and disable traditional school services, parents will resort to charter schools and vouchers. School districts and states compete for education resources tied to the federal government, which supports increasing the number of charter schools. There is no incentive for school districts to work together creatively.

In 2014, President Obama appointed NewSchools Venture Fund's CEO Ted Mitchell as Under Secretary of Education. Such an appointment sent another clear message that the president's agenda lay in privatizing America's public schools. Mitchell has supported and sits on an abundance of boards for groups that are considered anti-public school, and the expectation was that he would advocate for more online learning and initiatives to privatize public schools (Fang, 2013).

## WALTON FAMILY FOUNDATION

The Walton's influence on privatization, and their negative position toward America's public schools, has been widely reported. It is seen as odd since both Sam Walton and his wife received a public school education, and one could say they exemplify a public school success story. They should have boosted traditional public schools. Instead, the Walton family has become a harsh driver of school reform.

In 2004, *Fortune* described how *A Nation at Risk* influenced Sam Walton's views, causing him to believe in competition, charter schools, and vouchers. When asked whether their efforts were to undermine public schools, the Walton's late son, John Walton, quipped, "Education is a $700-plus-billion-a-year industry. By additive and incremental spending you are not going to move that environment. We aren't trying to change public schools, we are trying to change the educational environment so that public schools have to change for the better."[15]

The Waltons in that same year had paid for sixty-two thousand scholarships (parents paid 50 percent of the tuition) for poor children to attend private schools through the Children's Scholarship Fund (CSF). When Walton money is spent on charter schools and religious and private school vouchers, it weakens and reshapes public schools, just as Wal-Mart's small-town commerce domination (Hopkins, 2004).

The CSF, a nonprofit founded in 1998 by the late John Walton and the late financier and school choice supporter Ted Forstmann, is found in most large cities and is designed to provide scholarships for alternative public schooling. The program pushes the message that public schools fail. The CSF began with a large group of advisors such as Barbara Bush, Henry Kissinger, Charles Rangel, Eli Broad, and many others (Children's Scholarship Fund Charlotte). Wall Street's Stanley Druckenmiller and actor Will

Smith were also on the CSF board. It is unclear who sits on the advisory board at this time.

After John Walton's 2005 death in a plane crash, the *Wall Street Journal* wrote a tribute to the Walton family and their philanthropic contributions. They reported that the largest amount of the family fortune went to charter schools and vouchers. The paper praised the family's attempts to improve public schools through competition (Editorial, 2005).

Afterward, the *Arkansas Times* announced that the Walton Family Foundation had donated $20 million to set up a new University of Arkansas Department of Educational Reform (Smith and Brantley, 2005). The Waltons had already given a matching grant donation of $300,000 to the school for undergraduate honors and endowed graduate positions. Those who worried about Walton ideology expressed concern about a college program dedicated to vouchers and charter schools. Reed Greenwood, dean of the College of Education at the time, quieted those fears.

Greenwood hired, however, voucher advocate Jay P. Greene, a senior fellow with the conservative Manhattan Institute for Policy Research, as the new department head. Never an educator, Greene writes articles and blogs critical of public schools. His writings are often not peer-reviewed or are reviewed by those with similar beliefs. Topics include educational certification, teacher incentives, school choice, and accountability and online schooling.

Looming questions surround the Waltons' philanthropy, especially relating to education. Why does the Foundation support tax policies undermining poor populations? This would appear, in the long run, to hurt Wal-Mart's earnings. It might be that the Waltons foresee a larger enterprise in the "Wal-Martization" of public schools.[16]

## BROAD FOUNDATION

> You have to be quick on your feet to keep up with new Broad projects to reform education.
>
> —Kathy Emery and Susan Ohanian[17]

Billionaire Eli Broad made his wealth through two Fortune 500 companies he created—KB Home and SunAmerica, Inc. He and his wife, Edythe, at the time of this writing, devote time, energy, and resources to education, science, and the arts in what they see as their mission. Broad's degree in accounting is from Michigan State University, and, like the Waltons, both he and his wife attended public schools in Detroit. Broad seems to believe, like Sam Walton, that public schools at some point went downhill.

In a 2009 *Forbes* interview, Broad said, "We used to be No. 1 in the world in terms of [high school] graduation rates. Now we rank 20th."[18] He failed to acknowledge the social inclusiveness surrounding public schools and the challenges such changes present—that is, civil rights issues surrounding *Brown v. Board of Education*, the problems of poverty, and special education.

Broad often maintains a low profile in the community, though he casts a wide net of influence on public schooling across the country. So much so that in 2009, Tom Vander Ark, the first business executive to be a school superintendent, and who once worked for the Gates Foundation, referred to a speech by President Obama on *Huffington Post*, exclaiming:

> Obama's speech sounded like Eli wrote it. It was about choice and charter schools, human capital and performance pay. It was right on message from pre-school to college. We've never had a Republican president that so clearly articulated a Republican strategy. Only it's the new Democrat strategy.[19]

In 2009, Broad secured a number of strategic senior staff positions in the Los Angeles Unified School District. Questions surrounding transparency and the direction of school changes raised concerns, but Superintendent Ramon Cortines still accepted Broad's help to convert struggling public schools into charter schools (Blume, 2009). Broad's foundation provided millions toward the effort, including the controversial takeover of Locke High School by Green Dot Charter School.

But Broad is not the only influential business mogul in Los Angeles. "School districts there have received almost $4.4 million through a grant from the Wasserman Foundation; a $1.2 million grant from the Walton Family Foundation pays for LAUD student scholarships to private schools; and the Hewlett and Ford foundations provide smaller amounts."[20] Cities across America include their own individual businesses and public school critics. In most places the Chamber of Commerce wields power when it comes to influencing state testing standards and condemning public schools.

Broad, like other philanthropists, favors programs such as Teach for America, New Leaders for New Schools, and the New Teacher Project. All appear designed to replace university-prepared and experienced educators. He also supports the NewSchools Venture Fund and charter schools.

Broad initiatives dismantle public schools in three ways. The programs through his foundation, as described on their website, include several groups. The Broad Academy promises to prepare individuals for leadership and managerial positions in schools. Having an education administration degree from an accredited university or teaching experience does not matter. Broad Fellows complete a residency in an urban setting. As of 2015, Broad Academy had graduated 160 Fellows.

Many who obtain Broad Residencies are from Teach for America, marketing, political science, business administration, economics, and the military. Few show experience working with children in public school classrooms. The program focuses on standards, testing, data collection, results, and *especially school transformation.*

The second program is the Broad Prize for Urban Education, which involves $1 million given to struggling school districts, specifically distributed to students for college scholarships. But school districts must follow Broad criteria to get the Broad Prize. They have to conform to Broad rules involving raising test scores, competition, and providing incentives.

The third part of Broad's public school involvement involves inviting elected school board members to attend the Broad Institute for School Boards. The Institute runs summer residential learning programs modeled after a program for new mayors and members of Congress and administered by the Harvard Kennedy School. They partner with the Center for Reform of School Systems and Reform Governance in Action (RGA).

Concern is that such outside involvement takes away the democratic participation of parents, teachers, and the community who elect the school board. But school boards sign on to Broad's involvement, especially when city budgets are dwindling. School changes reflect Broad's ideology, often with little parent and/or community input.

Not only do Broad trainees move into influential positions in local school districts, they can be found working in the US Department of Education. Neil Campbell, education program analyst in the Office of Planning, Evaluation, and Policy Development, advised Arne Duncan on policy development and review; Kandace Jones was chief of staff in the Office of Elementary and Secondary Education; Donald Mitchell was special assistant for management systems in the Office of the Deputy Secretary; and Larkin Tackett was the special assistant to the assistant deputy secretary for innovation and improvement.

Another Broad Fellow, Thelma Melendez de Santa Ana, was assistant secretary for elementary and secondary education, and in 2014 moved to LA to be education advisor to the mayor there. She is the only one who listed education training and experience, although her degree is not in education.

Sometime around 2009, those who follow Broad's meddling with public schools and school districts learned of a guide called a "Tool Kit" titled *School Closure Guide: Closing Schools as a Means for Addressing Budgetary Challenges*. The guidebook, said to have been "developed by district operators with support from the Broad Foundation," is a detailed plot to excess (fire) teachers and generate community support for the destruction of their own public school system.[21]

In 2015, the *Los Angeles Times* acquired a forty-four-page proposal called "The Great Public Schools Now Initiative." The plan, organized through the Eli and Edythe Broad Foundation, would create 260 charters—enough to enroll 130,000 students in Los Angeles—shuttering traditional public schools. The proposal would include fund-raising by various foundations, and it would cost $490 million (Blume, 2015). Eli Broad's heavy influence on education, along with the Waltons and other business tycoons, is only outdone by another oligarch—Bill Gates.

## BILL AND MELINDA GATES FOUNDATION

> In light of the size of the foundation's endowment, Bill Gates is now the nation's superintendent of schools. He can support whatever he wants, based on any theory or philosophy that appeals to him. We must all watch for signs and portents to decipher what lies in store for American education.
>
> —Diane Ravitch, *Los Angeles Times*[22]

Many Americans see Bill and Melinda Gates as well-endowed philanthropists who want to help fix problematic schools and school districts. And, one assumes, that is how the Gates see themselves. When they chose Memphis, Tennessee, as a recipient of a Gates grant totaling $90,000,000, the school district brought out cheerleaders and school bands to celebrate. Philanthropists take on the role of hero to communities whose school districts experience serious budget cuts.

The Bill and Melinda Gates Foundation focuses on charter schools and teacher effectiveness, and more recently has been a strong backer of the Common Core State Standards and online instruction. Its influence is far-reaching in almost every area of public schooling. Few discussions about public schools take place without mentioning the Gates's involvement. Teachers and parents, however, are often not a part of changes that affect the school, and this raises serious questions.

The Gates's school initiatives in Memphis, for example, have involved teacher effectiveness and has included promoting controversial performance evaluations based on the use of Value-Added Measurement (VAM). The evaluation system has been used to fire teachers, using student test scores to rate teachers; this has been highly controversial.

Most teachers are distrustful of VAM because they realize other variables could affect student test results and the evaluation system has been set up poorly. VAM is especially troublesome for teachers who work with students who have learning challenges, students with disabilities, or students who have English as a second language.

In 2012, the Chicago Teachers Union went on strike, largely due to the evaluation system there. Teachers feared the closing of schools to make way for charter schools, and they did not want to lose their jobs due to test scores. Many of these teachers worked in high-poverty schools. With VAM, there is little, if any, consideration of the poor living conditions of students or other variables.

Cities receiving money from the Gates Foundation wind up with teacher quality and teacher effectiveness initiatives. But the Gates Foundation supports groups such as Teach for America and the New Teachers Project, so teachers may lose their jobs when schools close and charters take over. Fast-track-trained teachers who rarely spend more than a couple of years in the classroom replace teachers.

The Gates Foundation sponsored the Measures of Effective Teaching (MET) project, which spent several years studying thousands of teachers in six school districts (Bill and Melinda Gates Foundation, 2013). From the results surrounding this project, they claimed that teachers are a more important factor than class size, school funding, and technology, and that teaching is complex. They sought to show the importance of test score gains, student surveys, and classroom observations.

A study supported by the National Education Policy Center found that while the MET project was a robust study, it also had flaws and would not add to the knowledge of what makes an effective teacher (Rothstein and Mathis, 2013).

In 2005, at the National Education Summit on High Schools, which Gates cofounded, he said:

> America's high schools are obsolete. By obsolete, I mean that our high schools—even when they're working exactly as designed—cannot teach our kids what they need to know today. . . . Today, only one-third of our students graduate from high school ready for college, work, and citizenship. . . . This isn't an accident or a flaw in the system; it is the system.[23]

Remarks made by Gates are always debatable, but there is little public debate. And that is the problem.

Gates financially supports various organizations too numerous to mention. One of the better known and more radical, however, is Stand for Children (or called by critics "Stand *on* Children"), whose representatives can be found in school districts, infiltrating PTA meetings and obtaining important positions on school planning boards. They masquerade as children's rights advocates but are in reality highly biased in favor of charter schools and privatization.

The group is especially anti-teachers union. In 2011, Fred Klonsky's education blog provided a video of Jonah Edelman, Stand's leader, discussing how they "outfoxed" the Illinois teachers union.[24]

With no formal teacher education or experience working with children, but with a bundle of money to dangle in front of school districts, the Bill and Melinda Gates Foundation affects schools on many levels. Gates partly masterminded the documentary *Waiting for Superman*, by *An Inconvenient Truth* filmmaker Davis Guggenheim. The documentary severely criticized public schools. The film also failed at the box office.

In *The Upside of Irrationality: The Unexpected Benefits of Defying Logic at Work and at Home*, Dan Ariely, a Duke behavioral economist, notes: "Frankly, I am often amazed by the audacity of the assumptions that businesspeople and politicians make, coupled with their seemingly unlimited conviction that their intuition is correct. But politicians and businesspeople are just people, with the same decision biases we all have and the types of decisions they make are just as susceptible to errors in judgment as medical decisions. So shouldn't it be clear that the need for systematic experiments in business and policy is just as great?"[25]

The media, however, rarely questions the Gates's involvement in public schooling. In a 2008 episode of *Meet the Press*, Tom Brokaw, discussing No Child Left Behind, asked Senator Claire McCaskill (D-MO) what Senator Barack Obama would do about teacher accountability if he became president.

Brokaw stated: "Just yesterday I heard Bill Gates, who's deeply involved in education reform in this country, say, 'No Child Left Behind has not been perfect, but it has been phenomenal for two reasons. It's pointed out that education in America desperately needs reform, and that accountability is an important part of that.'"[26] Brokaw made no mention of the huge debate surrounding NCLB or the many Americans who believed its purpose included the destruction of public schools.

In 2005, *New York Times* writer Thomas L. Friedman, in *The World Is Flat: A Brief History of the Twenty-First Century*, describes Gates as a believer in the rote learning found in China and India. "When I asked Bill Gates about the supposed American education advantage—an education that stresses creativity, not rote learning—he was utterly dismissive. In his view, those who think that the more rote learning systems of China and Japan can't turn out innovators who can compete with Americans are sadly mistaken."[27]

But American ingenuity and creativity have been envied around the world. And though not entirely Gates's fault, public schools increasingly focus on rote learning (i.e., test prep, direct instruction, and rigid behavior) and less creative thinking and teaching to the whole child (elimination of the arts).

In 2006, Bill and Melinda Gates appeared on *The Oprah Winfrey Show*, one of the many times Gates can be found criticizing America's public schools. At the time of this writing, you could still find the discussion on Winfrey's website under the initial heading "America the Beautiful" and subheading "Failing Grade." They espoused this message: "Schools would be bankrupt" if run like a business.[28] This interview took place before America bailed out AIG, Goldman Sachs, and GM.

On the *Oprah* show, Melinda Gates said, "This [referring to the so-called crisis] is affecting all schools," though Oprah's show goes on to describe extreme disparities between a rich school in suburban Illinois and a poor school in Chicago.[29] Oprah's program provides accolades for KIPP charter school founders Mike Feinberg and Dave Levin. She would host Bill Gates again in 2010 to plug *Waiting for Superman.*

The Bill and Melinda Gates Foundation provides grants, like other foundations, to publications such as *Education Week.* They are contributors to National Public Television and have been connected with NBC's *Education Nation*. Melinda Gates sat on the board of the *Washington Post* until her resignation in 2010.

Yet the news isn't always forthcoming about Gates's school experimentation projects having less than favorable results. The closest they have come to introspection is 2006 when *Business Week* published an article titled "Bill

Gates Gets Schooled," describing the foundation's difficulties setting up small schools in Denver.

The break-up of large Manual High School into smaller schools failed in part because the smaller schools offered fewer courses. Students fled to schools where more classes were offered, and they left problematic students behind. Gates himself admitted that the business of schooling was not easy. Although the Gates Foundation charitable funding is included in such projects, failure costs taxpayers money too.

The small schools initiative wasn't the only project to run into trouble. In 2006, the Philadelphia School of the Future (SOF), a $63 million venture between Microsoft and Philadelphia's school district, debuted with fanfare. By 2009, *eSchool News* published a troubling report by the conservative American Enterprise Institute describing the serious problems surrounding the school. The SOF is described in more detail in the chapter about virtual education. Unlike traditional public schools that would have been shuttered, the SOF sought revamping.

Like Eli Broad, the education ideology of Bill Gates is entrenched in the US Department of Education (USDOE). Margot Rogers served as Education Secretary Arne Duncan's chief of staff after having previously worked with the Gates Foundation. Rogers eventually left that position and joined the Parthenon Group in 2011, where she is, at the time of this writing, vice chairman and senior advisor for education practice. She also sits on related boards and advisory commissions, including the Joyce Foundation and review boards for the Broad Prize for Urban Education and charter schools. Rogers has a JD from the University of Virginia School of Law, and a background in history. She lists no teaching experience.

James H. Shelton III, who was the USDOE's assistant deputy secretary for innovation and improvement, served as education program director for the Bill and Melinda Gates Foundation and has worked with the NewSchools Venture Fund. He cofounded LearnNow, a school management program acquired by Whittle's Edison Schools.

He also worked with McKinsey and Company, a business management consulting firm, advising CEOs on business strategy, and launched educational businesses through Michael Milken's Knowledge Universe, Inc. Shelton has a degree in computer science and a master's degree in business administration and education, but lists no teaching experience. In 2014, he was confirmed as deputy secretary of education for the US Department of Education.

What raises most questions is the disassociation of the public—parents and citizens—with their public schools. In 2006, David C. Bloomfield, professor and parent member of the New York Citywide Council on High Schools, wrote, "The most troubling aspects of the Gates program are its failure to engage in any semblance of public accountability, its history of secret evaluations, and its disowning of responsibility for the harm it has caused."[30]

## HIGH-STAKES TESTING

> The deeper tragedy is the loss of values traditionally celebrated by American education—values that helped make America the most prosperous and advanced nation in the world.
>
> —Yong Zhao[31]

When corporations rooted themselves in educational development planning via the New American Schools, standardization and testing took center stage. In the name of accountability, student test scores now measure schools. When those scores are low, which is often the case with poor public schools, the public school is shuttered, and it is replaced with a charter school that promises better test results. In general, public schools are condemned for their test scores whether it is justified or not.

The Program for International Student Assessment (PISA) is an international assessment measuring a fifteen-year-old's progress in basic school subjects. It has been administered every three years since 2000 (National Center for Education Statistics). The use of PISA scores to compare America's public schools is unfair. The media portrays education in this country as in crisis, falling behind other countries. The reality is that the United States has a higher poverty rate compared to other countries, and this makes comparisons difficult (Berliner and Glass, 2014, 12–17).

The National Assessment of Educational Progress (NAEP), a randomly administered assessment given in grades four, eight, and twelve, is also used to criticize public school students. Diane Ravitch, who was appointed to the NAEP board during the Clinton administration, says of the test, "Every time I hear elected officials or pundits complain about test scores, I want to ask them to take the same tests and publish their scores. I don't expect that any of them would accept the challenge."[32]

Ravitch charted slow, but steady and significant, progress in America's students, but the test results are often used to negatively discuss student test results. Similarly, Trends in International Mathematics and Science Study (TIMSS) has involved international testing comparisons in which America's students are portrayed in a bad light. But according to Ravitch, students do "surprisingly well."[33]

While some testing is justified and important to understanding student growth, few would dispute that the obsession with high-stakes testing has gone too far. Standardized testing is now a megamillion for-profit industry all its own, and many question not only its purpose but also the damage it is doing to both education and the children themselves.

High-stakes testing weakens curriculum and causes unnecessary stress among students. The overuse of data for questionable commercial purposes has also come under fire, and the country has seen an increased number of cheating scandals, the most infamous being in Atlanta.

As a result of high-stakes testing and a bar continually raised to developmentally inappropriate levels, students will eventually fail. Testing has become so draconian that even students with severe disabilities are administered harmful tests. When students fail, those in favor of privatization can blame teachers and public schools for unsuccessful results.

High-stakes testing is also being used to get rid of experienced and credentialed teachers who have risen to the top of the pay scale. Value-Added Measurement (VAM) is the controversial method to use student test scores to evaluate teachers. Researchers recognize that VAM is not fair to teachers. Some states are attempting to end this evaluation practice, but Race to the Top endorses it. In some places, teachers are seeking legal counsel on this issue.

High-stakes testing has led to concerns about an overemphasis on data collection. In the past, student information was tucked away in a file folder in a locked cabinet in the guidance office. With technology, access to student information becomes easier. This, along with changes to the Family Educational Rights and Privacy Act, has created privacy concerns for parents.

Parents, disgusted with the overemphasis on tests, will remove their children from public school if they can. This changes the overall dynamics of the public school population because wealthier students will no longer work side by side with poorer students. In the long run, this could significantly change how students view each other socially and lead to more class separation. The increase of testing has occurred over time in a calculated way to destroy public schooling.

## COMMON CORE STATE STANDARDS

The story of the corporate involvement involving Common Core State Standards (CCSS) starts in 2008. According to a 2014 report in the *Washington Post*, Gene Wilhoit, who was then executive director of the Council of Chief State School Officers, and standard's advocate David Coleman approached the Gates Foundation to see if Gates would bankroll the Common Core development (Layton, 2014). Gates and wife Melinda agreed, giving money to the following organizations to support the cause:

- American Federation of Teachers
- National Education Association
- US Chamber of Commerce
- Center for American Progress (liberal)
- American Legislative Exchange Council (conservative)
- State and local groups

One of the biggest supporters of CCSS is former Florida Republican governor Jeb Bush. Bush started the nonprofit Foundation for Excellence in Education that has, at the time of this writing, received $5.2 million from the Gates Foundation since 2010. Bush's education reforms are met with mixed reviews.

CCSS replaces state-created standards across the country. The creation of the standards is attributed to the National Governors Association and the Council of Chief State School Officers. Many state school officers come from Teach for America or the Broad Leadership Center.

The Gates Foundation is largely behind the CCSS. Concerns are that the standards have not been validated. Governors signed on to such drastic measures with little feedback from communities. Many conservative groups including the Tea Party and some liberals have expressed dissatisfaction over the Common Core. But Democrats have been critics too.

Oklahoma, South Carolina, and Louisiana have repealed CCSS, while states such as Indiana claim they are getting rid of them but are actually only changing the format of the original plan. Some states keep Common Core but change its name or the way it is implemented. Florida calls Common Core Florida Common Standards. Tennessee put CCSS on hold, but only temporarily.

Achieve is a Gates-backed nonprofit that emphasizes college attendance and heavily pushes the standards. Achieve has the backing of many corporations, including:

- Alcoa Foundation
- AT&T Foundation
- The Battelle Foundation
- Bill and Melinda Gates Foundation
- The Boeing Company
- Brookhill Foundation
- Carnegie Corporation of New York
- Chevron
- The Cisco Foundation
- DuPont
- The GE Foundation
- GSK
- IBM Foundation
- Intel Foundation
- The Joyce Foundation
- JPMorgan Chase Foundation
- The Leona and Harry B. Helmsley Charitable Trust
- Lumina Foundation
- MetLife Foundation
- The Prudential Foundation
- Sandler Foundation
- State Farm Insurance Companies
- Travelers Foundation
- The William and Flora Hewlett Foundation[34]

CCSS resembles the philosophical viewpoints of E. D. Hirsh. Hirsh's ideas center on education facts and concepts he believes important. Many considered him an elitist in the 1980s when his ideology first became known, but the CCSS are now seen as vindication of his work (Baker, 2013). His book *Cultural Literacy: What Every American Needs to Know* spawned books for every grade level, titled *What Your [Grade Level] Grader Needs to Know*.

While those behind CCSS claim it to be in-depth learning, it measures bits and pieces of information and aligns skills to standards. For example, close reading breaks down book passages with specified questions. There is no variation concerning student expectations, although how students reach the goals can be differentiated.

Student testing with Common Core State Standards involves two assessments. The Partnership for Assessment of Readiness for College and Careers (PARCC) is described as "The Next Generation . . . of Assessment," and the tests are promoted as tests to "assess students' current performance, and point the way to what students need to learn by graduation so they are ready for college or career."[35] But, like Common Core, the PARCC is highly controversial, and there are concerns about what and how it measures students. Also, how will the test affect students who fail (Horowitz, 2015)?

Smarter Balanced Assessment Consortium (SBAC) is an online assessment aligned to the Common Core State Standards. The test is supposed to help teachers check on student success. Concerns have been raised about the excessive difficulty of the questions, and there have been problems with student difficulty in using the computer for the SBAC testing.

The idea of common goals for all raises questions concerning students with disabilities. That all students should learn the same information conflicts with devising an Individual Educational Plan. For students with unique needs, Common Core supporters promote assistive learning, but there is nothing concrete to assure students with disabilities that they have a safety net if they fail the test.

Many parents and educators resent the Gates Foundation for being involved with school standards, and conservatives especially accuse those behind the standards of creating a national school agenda that overrides states' rights. Gates, and other CCSS advocates, such as Jeb Bush, have tried to justify CCSS, but serious concerns surrounding lacking involvement of teachers in creating the standards is a source of contention. Common Core supporters often reference the teachers unions as being on board for Common Core. When it comes to the leadership of those unions, they are correct.

## TEACHERS UNIONS

> If we use these common standards as the foundation for better schools, we can give all kids a robust curriculum taught by well-prepared, well supported teacher[s] who can help prepare them for success in college, life and careers.
> —Randi Weingarten[36]

States with strong teachers unions—Massachusetts, Connecticut, and New Jersey—are states that have seen strong test scores in the past. But the leadership of the American Federation of Teachers (AFT) and the National Education Association (NEA) have alienated some of their members by accepting money from the Bill and Melinda Gates Foundation and other reform groups.

While there have been rallies—namely, the uprising in Madison, Wisconsin, against Governor Scott Walker in 2011, and the Chicago teachers' strike in 2012—concern has been voiced by teachers who worry that national union leaders have sided with the very groups they are supposed to fight against.

Both AFT president Randi Weingarten and former NEA president Dennis Van Roekel voiced support in favor of Race to the Top, Value-Added Measurement for teacher evaluations, merit pay, Teach for America credentialing, and charter schools. More recently, they have found favor with Common Core State Standards. This has raised doubts on the part of millions of educators who desire a union that reflects their best interests and not corporate reforms.

Nowhere was the rift between teachers and union leaders more apparent than when Weingarten invited Bill Gates to speak at the 2010 AFT convention in Seattle. The YouTube video of the event shows an enthusiastic Weingarten introduction met with boos from the crowd. But some teachers also appeared accepting of Weingarten's message and Gates himself.

Weingarten has also repeatedly been a panel guest on NBC's *Education Nation*, seen as biased by many educators who bemoan the lack of representation of speakers who support public education. It is seen more as a platform for Bill Gates and corporate CEOs to get school privatization propaganda across to the American people.

Like Weingarten, Van Roekel also supported the Common Core State Standards and promoted them until his retirement from the NEA. The NEA website is full of reports pitching the CCSS to teachers and parents. Van Roekel claimed the standards were not initiated properly—that their rollout was flawed (Van Roekel, 2014). This subtly shifts the blame to the teachers, implying that *they* are not able to implement the standards successfully. But many educators and parents do not like the CCSS.

While corporations have never been fond of unions, the list of corporate donors to teachers unions is long, which raises questions. The AFT donor list includes:

- The Actuarial Foundation

- The Bill and Melinda Gates Foundation
- The Carnegie Corporation
- Charles Lafitte Foundation
- The Charles Stuart Mott Foundation
- Citigroup Foundation
- The Coca-Cola Foundation
- The Eli Broad Foundation
- The Ford Foundation
- The Joyce Foundation
- W. K. Kellogg Foundation
- The Pew Charitable Trusts
- RGK Foundation
- The Spencer Foundation
- The Wallace Foundation [37]

The NEA also has its share of corporate donors, including the Bill and Melinda Gates Foundation, who in 2013 contributed $3,882,600 to "support a cohort of National Education Association Master Teachers in the development of Common Core-aligned lessons in K–5 mathematics and K–12 English Language Arts."[38] Lily Eskelsen García became the new NEA president in 2014, and while her initial speech proved fiery, she continues the same message that CCSS were not rolled out appropriately. She appears to believe in the Common Core State Standards.

## AMERICAN LEGISLATIVE EXCHANGE COUNCIL

The Bill and Melinda Gates Foundation supports a variety of anti-public school groups, and mostly such donating goes unchallenged by the general public. In 2012, they withdrew their support from the American Legislative Exchange Council (ALEC). Several corporations pulled their support, along with the Gates Foundation, due to the group's support of the Stand Your Ground law and controversy surrounding the law and the shooting of a Florida teenager.

ALEC is a powerful, corporate-backed, mostly Republican group, pushing a variety of controversial measures that permeate society. Education is the area where the Gates Foundation seemed most interested. They had contributed $376,635 to support ALEC's causes concerning education (Clawson, 2011). ALEC sees education as a battle for free market schools and vouchers.

The Milton Friedman Foundation is at the center of their beliefs and their fight.

The power and influence on public policy by ALEC is secretive. Meetings are usually closed. ALEC is influential in pushing controversial education reforms that restructure schools in a direct effort meant to remove governmental funding, and that includes creating vouchers for students with disabilities (Underwood, 2011).

For twenty years, ALEC's efforts have been to privatize public schools through vouchers, charter schools, and technology. ALEC supports other issues such as merit pay, single-sex education, school uniforms, and political and religious indoctrination of students (Beilke, 2012).

In 2012, state legislators met at the Ritz Carlton, on remote Amelia Island, near Jacksonville. The gathering excluded the public—students, parents, teachers, and the press. Questions were raised as to why the most crucial individuals in education would be omitted from the meeting, especially since ALEC has been promoted as transparent on their website.

While Bill Gates may have stepped away from ALEC, he and other wealthy philanthropists and education reformers have had their own meeting. Gates, along with Jeb Bush, Oprah, previous mayor of New York Michael Bloomberg, Warren Buffett, Cleveland Cavaliers owner Dan Gilbert, and other billionaires met at South Carolina's posh Kiawah Island. On *60 Minutes*, Bill and Melinda Gates described the new group as signing on to a giving pledge. These meetings were also closed to the public but appeared to include education planning (Rose, 2013).

ALEC and outside groups influence state legislators who plan public school policy impacting local school districts. They do this increasingly without the input of their constituents—those whose children attend public schools. They ignore sunshine laws that have been in existence for years. Many of the decisions and policies these groups champion are not based on adequate research.

Consider the parent "trigger" bill, one of the controversial initiatives advanced by ALEC. The idea is that if parents are not happy with their schools, they can, through a petition, shut down a public school and reopen it as a charter school. It is deceptive because it makes parents feel as if they have power when they are handing their schools over to for-profit charter school managers.

Parent Revolution founder and Green Dot charter school aficionado Ben Austin leads the California Walton-backed idea. Austin is a millionaire with no formal educational credentials and, at the time of this writing, no children in public schools. The parent trigger is a serious ploy to privatize public schools and was the subject of the 2012 corporate-backed movie *Won't Back Down*.

Though serious concerns surround the parent trigger law, it has been backed by Education Secretary Arne Duncan, Michelle Rhee, Governor Jeb Bush, and the other education reformers. In 2012, members of the Florida Legislature came together to back a Parent Trigger bill, but the Florida PTA, League of Women Voters, Parents Across America, Save Duval Schools, and Facebook groups called 50th No More and Testing Is Not Teaching came together to stop the bill. But support for the Parent Trigger bill is still strong in some places, and the supporters are aggressive.

## CONCLUSION: AMERICA'S SCHOOLS

While it may seem impossible to fight against wealth and harmful ideology for good public schools, grassroots organizations are making the attempt and seeing success. These groups include educators, parents, students, and community members who recognize the importance of public education. Most of the serious reform pushback comes against high-stakes testing, since these tests are used to condemn teachers, schools, and students.

In the summer of 2011, a new organization called Save Our Schools marched in Washington, DC. It was the first time teachers and parents from around the country came together to advocate for public schools and against harmful reforms. In 2012, the organization met again to plan strategies for future activism.

The National Opt Out group was born from the Save Our Schools march. It encourages and supports parents to opt their students out of unnecessary high-stakes tests since tests are used to close schools, fire teachers, and are harmful to children. United Opt Out has gained acceptance by parents and teachers searching for a way to make public schools more meaningful and less stressful.

By opting students out of the test, parents reduce the importance of high-stakes testing. This is not a perfect solution. School officials sometimes punish children who sit the test out. But it is currently one of the few solutions to fight against harmful testing. If more parents and teachers opted out, there would be no more reason to administer harmful tests! Opting out of the test is especially successful when there is a concerted effort by groups of parents and teachers to come together to say no to high-stakes testing.

In 2013, teachers at Garfield High School in the Seattle School District unanimously boycotted the Measures of Academic Progress (MAP) test (Micucci, 2013). Students and parents backed their effort, and eventually the number of schools opting out of the test in that school district grew to seven. Garfield stands as an example for schools across the country to follow.

In 2014, the Lee County School Board in Florida, with the support of parents and teachers, voted to opt students out of high-stakes testing. Later, a school board member rescinded his vote, permitting testing to continue, but the actions of the board and the media attention that it involved brought attention to the issue of high-stakes testing in Florida and across the country. Many school districts are now reconsidering the tests.

While all of these actions have not been successful to end high-stakes testing altogether, the momentum is growing. In 2015, 20 percent of New York's students opted out of the test. When 200,000 third- through eighth-graders sit out of a state test, it is seen as a mark of growing resistance (Harris, 2015). New York was not alone. Many states saw a decrease in students taking the tests.

A group called the Bad Ass Teachers Association (BATs) has successfully galvanized many teachers and parents to fight *together* against harmful school reform. Many of the BATs teachers work within their union organizations to support the cause of good public schooling for all students. The group has a respected blog and Facebook pages around the world.

The Network for Public Education builds alliances with grassroots groups across the country to oppose school privatization, high-stakes testing, and other harmful reforms. They also support a variety of positive principles and actions for public schools, which include addressing class size. Diane Ravitch, Anthony Cody, Carol Burris, and other educational activists maintain the program.

While using standardized tests to evaluate teachers is controversial and unproven, it is still used by many school districts. Newspapers in places such as Los Angeles and Florida have published teacher VAM scores and have made them available to the public. But in places such as Tennessee, teachers have filed lawsuits against pay-for-performance plans that use Value-Added Measurement (Sawchuk, 2014).

In Florida, anger erupted in February 2014 when the mother of a developmentally disabled student was asked to write an excuse to get her child out of the Alternate Florida Comprehensive Assessment Test (FCAT). Ethan Rediske, who had severe disabilities, lay dying, but his mother, Andrea Rediske, had to plead with the school district to let him bypass the test (McGrory and Solocheck, 2014). Rediske courageously spoke out against such insensitive testing.

Testing has become mandatory for all students with disabilities. The outrage surrounding Ethan was great enough to put pressure on the legislature to introduce a bill to outlaw testing for students with severe disabilities. The bill ultimately failed, but no one will forget Ethan or his brave mother.

In 2012, the Chicago Teachers Union went on strike due to the destructive policies put forth by Democratic mayor Rahm Emanuel. The strike brought attention to the draconian attacks on teachers and public schools across the country. But Chicago still faces challenges that are not easily overcome.

Republicans and Democrats have surprisingly come together to address Common Core State Standards. Parents Across America provides an outlet for parents and teachers to speak out on questionable school policy. Most groups want local involvement and community ownership of their public schools.

Organizations such as Save Our Schools and BATS also start branches in states and within local communities. State and regional groups such as Tennessee Reclaiming Educational Excellence (TREE) and Tennessee Parents provide forums for conversation and activism.

Along with fighting for good education policy, working together to actively reject harmful policies is important. Professor and dean of the School of Education at the University of Wisconsin-Madison, Julie Underwood, along with Julie F. Mead, professor and chair of the Department of Educational Leadership and Policy Analysis, also at the University of Wisconsin-Madison, provide a set of questions pertaining to legislation and the troubling ALEC initiatives.

These questions should be asked when addressing any new school proposal—local, state, or federal—that school reformers attempt to impose upon public schools. The questions include:

- Is the sponsor a member of ALEC?
- Does the bill borrow from ALEC model legislation?
- What corporations had a hand in drafting the legislation?
- What interests would benefit or even profit from its passage?

The most important recommended point is to question "whether ALEC's influence builds or undermines democracy."[39] This question can be asked about any reform measure.

Americans do not want to lose their public schools. They have come to realize that the changes due to current corporate reforms are not best for America's children. The fight across America is to put the "public" back into public schools.

## NOTES

1. *A Nation at Risk: The Imperative for Educational Reform: A Report to the Nation and the Secretary of Education, United States Department of Education* (Washington, DC: National Commission on Excellence in Education, 1983), 5.
2. *A Nation At Risk.*
3. Harold Howe, II, "Sins of Omission in 'America,'" *Education Digest* 57, no. 29 (1992): 4.
4. Maris A. Vinovskis, *The Road to Charlottesville: The 1989 Education Summit* (National Education Goals Panel, September 1999).
5. Margaret Spillane and Bruce Shapiro, "A Small Circle of Friends: Bush's New American Schools (New American Schools Development Corp.) (Cover Story)," *The Nation*, September 21, 1992.
6. Ibid.
7. Kenneth J. Saltman, *The Edison Schools: Corporate Schooling and the Assault on Public Education* (New York: Routledge, 2005), 15.
8. David C. Berliner and Bruce J. Biddle, *The Manufactured Crisis: Myths, Fraud, and the Attack on America's Public Schools* (Cambridge, MA: Perseus Books, 1995), 166.
9. Robert M. Huelskamp, "Perspectives on Education in America," *Phi Delta Kappan* 74, no. 9 (1993): 718–21.
10. Daniel Tanner, "A Nation 'Truly' at Risk," *Phi Delta Kappan* 75, no. 4 (1993): 288–91.
11. William Clinton, "President Clinton Urges Standards That Count. Excerpts from President Clinton's Address to the National Education Summit," *American Educator* 20, no. 1 (1996): 8–12.
12. Stephen Metcalf, "Reading Between the Lines," *The Nation*, January 10, 2002.
13. Ibid.
14. James Flanigan, "Venture Capitalists Are Investing in Educational Reform," *New York Times*, February 16, 2006.
15. Andy Serwer, "The Waltons: Inside America's Richest Family," *Fortune* 150, no. 10 (November 15, 2004).
16. Betty Feng and Jeff Krehely, "The Waltons and Wal-Mart Self-Interested Philanthropy," National Committee for Responsive Philanthropy, September 2005, http://reclaimdemocracy.org/walmart/walton_philanthropy.pdf.
17. Kathy Emery and Susan Ohanian, *Why Is Corporate America Bashing Our Public Schools?* (Portsmouth, NH: Heinemann, 2004), 90.
18. Michael Maiello, "Debriefing Eli Broad," *Forbes*, March 7, 2009, http://www.forbes.com/2009/03/19/aig-eli-broad-intelligent-investing-broad.html.

19. Tom Vander Ark, "Eli Finally Won," Huffington Post, May 25, 2011, http://www.huffingtonpost.com/tom-vander-ark/eli-finally-won_b_174152.html.

20. Howard Blume, "Key L.A. Unified Staff Positions Are Funded Privately," *Los Angeles Times*, December 16, 2009.

21. "School Closure Guide: Closing Schools as a Means for Addressing Budgetary Challenges," The Broad Foundation Education (and District Operators), updated September 15, 2009, http://failingschools.files.wordpress.com/2011/01/school-closure-guide1.pdf.

22. Diane Ravitch, "Bill Gates, the Nation's Superintendent of Schools," *Los Angeles Times*, July 30, 2006.

23. "Bill Gates—National Education Summit on High Schools," February 26, 2005, prepared remarks by Bill Gates, cochair, Bill and Melinda Gates Foundation, http://www.gatesfoundation.org/speeches-commentary/Pages/bill-gates-2005-national-education-summit.aspx.

24. "Stand for Children's Jonah Edelman Explains How They Out Foxed Illinois Teacher Union Leadership," Fred Klonsky Education Blog, July 7, 2011, http://preaprez.wordpress.com/2011/07/07/stand-for-childrens-jonah-edelman-explains-how-they-out-foxed-illinois-teacher-union-leadership/.

25. Dan Ariely, *The Upside of Irrationality: The Unexpected Benefits of Defying Logic at Work and at Home* (New York: HarperCollins, 2010), 292–93.

26. *Meet the Press*, July 13, 2008, http://www.msnbc.msn.com/id/25662958/.

27. Thomas L. Friedman, *The World Is Flat: A Brief History of the Twenty-First Century* (New York: Farrar, Straus and Giroux, 2005), 264–65.

28. *The Oprah Winfrey Show*, "America the Beautiful. Failing Grade," April 11, 2006, http://www.oprah.com/world/Failing-Grade/slide_number/2#slide.

29. Ibid.

30. David C. Bloomfield, "Come Clean on Small Schools," *Education Week* 25, no. 20 (2006): 34–35.

31. Yong Zhao, *Who's Afraid of the Big Bad Dragon? Why China Has the Best (and Worst) Educational System in the World* (San Francisco, CA: Jossey-Bass, 2014), 5.

32. Diane Ravitch, *Reign of Error: The Hoax of the Privatization Movement and the Danger to America's Public Schools* (New York: Alfred A. Knopf, 2014), 44–54.

33. Ibid., 66.

34. Achieve, Our Contributors, http://www.achieve.org/contributors.

35. PARCC, The PARCC Tests, http://www.parcconline.org/about/the-parcc-tests.

36. Council of Chief State School Officers Press Release, "National Governors Association and State Education Chiefs Launch Common State Academic Standards," June 2, 2014, http://www.ccsso.org/News_and_Events/Press_Releases/NATIONAL_GOVERNORS_ASSOCIATION_AND_STATE_EDUCATION_CHIEFS_LAUNCH_COMMON_STATE_ACADEMIC_STANDARDS_.html.

37. AFT, Foundation Funds, http://www.aft.org/education/well-prepared-and-supported-school-staff/school-improvement/foundation-funds.

38. The NEA Foundation for the Improvement of Education, "How We Work Grant," Bill and Melinda Gates Foundation, http://www.gatesfoundation.org/How-We-Work/Quick-Links/Grants-Database/Grants/2013/07/OPP1092055.

39. Julie Underwood and Julie F. Mead, "A Smart ALEC Threatens Public Education," *Phi Delta Kappan* 93, no. 6 (2012): 51–55.

## *Chapter Two*

# Replacing Public Schools with Charter Schools

> "I know right now, and the answer's no. No, doggone it! You sit around here and you spin your little webs and you think the whole world revolves around you and your money! Well, it doesn't, Mr. Potter! In the, in the whole vast configuration of things, I'd say you were nothing but a scurvy little spider!"
>
> —George Bailey in *It's a Wonderful Life*

## LOST OPPORTUNITY

In the early 1970s, Ray Budde, a teacher/principal turned college professor for educational administration, wrote a thesis about creating educational innovation in school districts. His plan called for teachers to work without bureaucratic oversight in small settings to try out innovative ideas (Budde, 1996).

Budde's colleagues showed little interest. But after *A Nation at Risk* and a Carnegie report calling for the redesign of public schools, he resubmitted his proposal for publication. This time it was published, and the idea caught the attention of the American Federation of Teachers (AFT) president Albert Shanker.

In 1988, Shanker introduced charter schools in a speech to the National Press Club. Like Budde, Shanker envisioned groups of teachers with parents working cooperatively to help children find and develop their interests. Charter schools would be smaller, focused on personalized learning, and likened to learning laboratories. Teachers, pioneering new approaches, would serve to create model programs of innovation.

Both Budde and Shanker believed charter schools would empower teachers. But before Shanker's death in 1997, he realized the original charter school concept had been stolen by those who wanted for-profit schools—including the religious right who saw charter schools as a means to get a foothold into public schooling, and those who disliked school integration wanted separate schools (Kahlenberg, 2007, 313–14). Shanker also worried about Chris Whittle's Edison schools.

The AFT described rules for charter schools. They would:

- Be tuition-free, not-for-profit, and open and accessible to all students on an equal basis.
- Operate transparently by fully disclosing their finances, curriculum, student demographics, and academic outcomes to parents and the public.
- Meet or exceed the same academic standards and assessment requirements that apply to other public schools.
- Hire well-qualified teachers.
- Work cooperatively with local school districts.
- Permit their employees to freely form unions.[1]

The AFT and the National Education Association (NEA) have been critical of charter schools. But they also support the old charter school concept.

Changes affecting public schools gradually became apparent to educators. Hillary Clinton exemplified the revelation when, in a 1999 speech to the NEA in Orlando, she surprised teachers by saying: "I stand behind the charter school/public school movement, because parents do deserve greater choice within the public school system to meet the unique needs of their children. Slowly but surely, we're beginning to create schooling opportunities through the public school charter system-raising academic standards, empowering educators. When we look back on the 1990s, we will see that the charter school movement will be one of the ways we will have turned around the entire public school system."[2]

Clinton, probably unintentionally (she was there for a Friend of Education Award), snubbed the audience of teachers from traditional public schools. Perhaps recognizing her faux pas, she quickly switched to condemning vouchers. But her speech demonstrated the growing chasm between traditional public schools and the charter school movement and teacher support by the Democratic Party.

The idea that charter schools help public schools has never been shown to be true. Teachers hired by charter operators usually have less professional preparation. Their salaries are reduced, and they often receive fewer benefits compared to teachers in traditional public schools. Charter schoolteachers can also expect to work longer hours and have less job security. Without union representation, they can be fired on a whim.

The 1990s saw a proliferation of charter schools, but many of those hired as teachers lacked credentials. By 2005, 45 percent of Ohio's 250 charter schoolteachers lacked full state certification—about the same as winning a coin flip (Stephens, 2005). Ohio's remaining traditional public schools, however, boasted 98 percent certification of subject area teachers. Those who criticize public schools still claim charter schools create innovation, but without experienced, qualified teachers, that seems hard to believe.

## NONPROFIT/FOR-PROFIT

According to the National Alliance for Public Charter Schools, "67 percent of all charter schools are independently run non-profit, single site schools; 20 percent are run by non-profit organizations that run more than one charter school; and just under 13 percent are run by for-profit companies. For-profit charter schools have to meet financial oversight regulations, just like any company the government contracts with to provide a service."[3]

But even as nonprofits, charter schools receive tax dollars diverted from traditional public schools. Whether nonprofit or for-profit, Americans pay taxes for charter schools, but they are run mostly without community or parental participation. This makes it difficult to tell how they are run and what they do.

Florida has been a bellwether state when it comes to for-profit charter schools. According to a 2002 report in the *St. Petersburg Times*, 75 percent of the 76,000 charter schools in Florida had become for-profits at that time (Fischer, 2002). Much of the charter school movement in Florida hinged on the beliefs of Jonathan Hage. Hage, a speechwriter for President H. W. Bush, worked for the conservative Heritage Foundation.

According to the same report, Chancellor charter school's stated revenue in 2001 was $100 million, mostly from state government grants, and the schools eventually united with Beacon Academies under the name Chancellor Beacon Academies. Dennis Bakke and his wife, who run Imagine Charter Schools, purchased Beacon. Miami-Dade County Superintendent Octavio Visiedo left his job and helped establish Chancellor Academies.

Once paid higher than any superintendent in the country, Visiedo opened charter schools in Florida, Arizona, and the District of Columbia. He served as executive vice president of Imagine Schools and is president of Chancellor Supplemental Educational Services, a tutorial company. Once referencing charter schools, he said, "The potential is endless. Charters will change the (public education) landscape forever. It's big business."[4] Imagine Schools are controversial. In *Hoosier School Heist*, Doug Martin outlines the Religious Right's business and political connections with these schools (2014, 106–9).

In 2007, a four-part *Orlando Sentinel* report on charter schools described the $1 billion industry. Florida Republican senator Don Gaetz, past school superintendent and chair of the education committee, expressed alarm over the speed at which charter schools were growing. He said, "They have lobbyists—they walk around in thousand-dollar suits, some of them. Some are still struggling, idealistic, mom-and-pop shops, and they need assistance. But the big boys and the mature organizations should be held accountable for how they use public money and how they educate children."[5]

The report describes how most charter schools lack oversight and have fewer regulations than traditional public schools. Students can be treated poorly. They fail tests in charter schools, and those schools suddenly close in the middle of a school year. Students in a Tampa charter school were denied diplomas when their charter school closed, yet the school later reopened in another school district.

Though no shortages of charter school scandals exist around the country, a number of them stand out in Florida. One example involved Escambia Charter School, which made a $200,000 profit contracting with the Florida Department of Education for students to cut roadside grass and weeds (McClure and Shanklin, 2007). Students received less pay than ordinary employees. Even after being exposed, the school remained open.

In 2011, Jonathan Hage was listed on the Foundation for Excellence in Education's website (Governor Jeb Bush's organization) as president and chief executive officer of Charter Schools USA. The foundation lists as its mission "to ignite a movement of reform, state by state, to transform education for the 21st century."[6] Hage, whose degrees are not in education, became Floridian of the Year for his management of the charter schools and their rapid development across the country (Rockwell, 2012).

Charter Schools USA, at the time of this writing, has fifty-one schools in Florida, two in Georgia, four in Illinois, three in Indiana, seven in Louisiana, one in Michigan, and three in North Carolina. In almost every city one finds charter schools, many for profit, replacing shuttered public schools.

More charter schools than traditional public schools can be found in places such as New Orleans and Philadelphia. Memphis is also fast becoming primarily a charter school district. Damning reports surrounding charter schools are being reported more frequently, but little is done to increase transparency.

In 2012 to 2013, the League of Women Voters of Florida examined the use of tax dollars allocated to charter schools in that state. While funding for traditional public schools was scarce, some charter school management companies turned a profit. Even when local school boards rejected charter schools, they were sometimes approved by the state. Charter schools had more teacher turnover. Many charters were segregated, and they failed to serve the poor. They were also selective in their admission and dismissal procedures. And many charter schools had poor financial management (2014).

In 2014, an investigation into Michigan's charter schools found lacking accountability and poor performance. Charter schools found to be failing remained open ten years or longer despite being responsible for more than 140,000 children (Dixon, 2014). Here is an example of Michigan charter school violations:

- A Sault Ste. Marie charter school board gave its administrator a severance package worth $520,000 in taxpayer money.
- A Bedford Township charter school spent more than $1 million on swampland.
- A mostly online charter school in Charlotte spent $263,000 on a Dale Carnegie confidence-building class, $100,000 more than it spent on laptops and iPads.
- Two board members who challenged their Romulus school's management company over finances and transparency were ousted when the length of their terms was summarily reduced by Grand Valley State University.
- National Heritage Academies, the state's largest for-profit school management company, charges fourteen of its Michigan schools $1 million or

more in rent—which many real estate experts say is excessive. A charter school in Pittsfield Township gave jobs and millions of dollars in business to multiple members of the founder's family.

- Charter authorizers have allowed management companies to open multiple schools without a proven track record of success.[7]

## CHARTER VERSUS PUBLIC SCHOOLS

School reformers claim charter schools are better than traditional public schools, but there is no proof of this. According to the 2003 National Assessment of Educational Progress, charter schools performed approximately a half a year behind in reading and math compared to students in traditional public schools. The report appeared in the *New York Times*, also detailing how the American Federation of Teachers (AFT) circulated the test results after the US Department of Education had procrastinated reporting outcomes (Schemo, 2004, 1). This set off a flood of rebuttals by charter school advocates.

Attempting damage control, US Secretary of Education Rod Paige, under President George W. Bush, challenged the report, claiming that charter schools were for poorer students with more problems and differences than students from traditional public schools (Schemo, 2004, 2).

Charter advocates, including Jeanne Allen of the Center for Education Reform, ran an ad worth $115,000 countering the claims of the report, and Harvard economist Caroline Hoxby denounced the findings, claiming she had found contrary results (Henig, 2008, 3). It later became apparent that Hoxby's statistics were faulty. She admitted to a problem with "downloading data from different Web sites."[8]

Another 2004 study found less achievement in North Carolina charter schools as compared to public schools. The researchers determined part of the problem to be a 30 percent negative effect of charter schools due to high turnover rates of students (Bifulco and Ladd, 2004). Questions arose as to why certain charter schools were chosen and whether parents had the ability to choose good charter schools.

In 2009, a report by the Center for Research on Education Outcomes (CREDO), from the Hoover Institution at Stanford University, determined a wide quality variance in charter schools across the country (Wolf and Browne, 2009). Charter school students did not fare as well as students in traditional public schools.

Caroline Hoxby, now at Stanford, tried again to challenge the negative results. She claimed the CREDO study contained "a serious statistical mistake that causes a negative bias in its estimate of how charter schools affect achievement."[9] CREDO researchers responded quickly: "The memo, 'A Serious Statistical Mistake in the CREDO Study of Charter Schools,' by Caroline Hoxby, does not provide any basis whatsoever for discounting the reliability of the CREDO study conclusions."[10]

Hoxby also presented a positive report on the success of New York City's charter schools in 2009. Educational researcher Gerald Bracey, reacting to the 2009 *Washington Post* editorial that praised Hoxby's research, said Hoxby is "the only person in the whole country who consistently finds results that favor charters."[11] In 2013, CREDO showed that charter schools had improved, but they still had not surpassed traditional public schools.

Many wonder why traditional public schools are compared to charter schools when the structure of charter schools and their student makeup differ widely. Charter schools often pick students randomly in lotteries, but after those drawings they require student behavior contracts and parent involvement. Students may be sent home if they do not follow school rules, misbehave, or fail tests (US Charter Schools). Students may be dismissed if parents are not involved. All of this is a process called "creaming," and such requirements are not part of traditional public schools. Such student selectivity gives charter schools a testing advantage. Still, charter schools are, as a whole, not succeeding as promised.

In *The Charter School Dust-Up*, authors from the Economic Policy Institute, examining charter schools, wrote:

> First, the evidence available shows that charter schools do not generate higher average student achievement than do regular public schools and, especially, have not improved the educational performance of central city, low-income minority children. Second, charter schools do not typically enroll the "disadvantaged of the disadvantaged" rather, the minority students enrolled in charter schools are no more likely to be low-income than those in other public schools. Third, charter schools seem to be associated with some increased segregation in schooling. Fourth, charter schools churn students more frequently than regular public schools, and the achievement of students often suffers when they change schools. Fifth, charter schools, through the introduction of competition, are not systematically leading other public schools to be better. (126)[12]

Despite controversy surrounding charter schools, in 2009, President Obama and Education Secretary Arne Duncan threatened to withhold millions in federal Race to the Top stimulus funds to states if they refused to remove caps on charter schools. Why do this when research indicates charter schools do no better than traditional public schools?

Instead of focusing on creating good public schools for all children, the objective appeared to be to eliminate traditional public schools—moving full-speed ahead toward privatization. But problems exist with this ideology that will not be solved easily.

## SEGREGATION

> The charter school movement has been a major political success, but it has been a civil rights failure.
>
> —Civil Rights Project/Proyecto Derechos Civiles[13]

Charter schools are sometimes favored by individuals we would consider civil rights activists. Al Sharpton and many African American parents along with President Obama support charter schools. They rally behind them as innovative and a great investment for students. This is puzzling because charter schools are often segregated. Charter schools reflect the kind of schools so many fought hard to eliminate through *Brown v. Board of Education*, the landmark US Supreme Court case that found separate public schools for black and white students was unconstitutional.

In 2010, the UCLA Civil Rights Project determined that charter schools *isolate students by race and class.*[14] Still, the number of charter schools almost tripled since 2000 to 2001.

Along with this, an analysis by the Education and Public Interest Center found Education Management Organization–operated charter schools, compared to the public school district in which the charter school resided, were more segregated by race and wealth, and they had fewer students with disabilities and English-Language Learners (Miron, Urschel, Mathis, and Tornquist, 2010). But federal, state, and local education agencies continue to fund charter schools that do not foster diversity.

The segregation problem is no less prevalent in Hispanic communities. Some 75 percent of students in California's Green Dot charter schools are Hispanic (US DOE). Founder Steve Barr received millions from Bill Gates and Eli Broad in support of Green Dot aggressively expanding in the Los

Angeles area. Barr is known for the Green Dot takeover in 2007 of Alain LeRoy Locke High School in Watts. Barr's group quietly obtained signatures from thirty-seven of the seventy-three tenured teachers, legally approving "a bare majority" according to author educator Susan Ohanian.[15]

After the turnover, fired teachers had to reapply for their jobs, and only 30 percent were rehired. The school, broken into eight small schools, and with additional private funding of $15 million, improved crime and school atmosphere. But test scores have not been stellar, and a scandal having to do with rundown bathrooms lacking privacy stalls for boys proved embarrassing (Ceasar, 2013).

Barr was no educator but a political shaker and mover. He cofounded Rock the Vote, financially chaired the Democratic Party, and hosted President Clinton's National Service Inaugural, which led to the creation of Americorp. US Education Secretary Arne Duncan expressed interest in committing several billion dollars to replicate a "Locke-style takeover" of troubled schools across the country. "You seem to have cracked the code," he told Barr.[16]

But when diversely populated Emerson Middle School, near Los Angeles, found itself on the verge of being closed and converted to another Green Dot Charter School, a teacher (in reference to parents organized by Green Dot's paid consultant, city official, and "parent trigger" supporter Ben Austin) said:

> Frankly, they are afraid of the very thing that the teachers, administrators, staff members, and neighborhood parents who choose to send their children to Emerson believe is one of our greatest assets: we are a true microcosm of Los Angeles. Thirty different languages are spoken on our campus. Our students are growing up without racial prejudices and cultural biases because they are personally familiar with the variety of cultures, sub-cultures and ethnicities that exist in this city—the very thing desegregation was to promote. Diversity is working on our campus![17]

*The San Francisco Examiner* compared Emerson's test scores with Green Dot. The Academic Performance Index (API), California's school achievement reporting system, indicated twelve of fifteen Green Dot schools as having APIs *lower* than diverse Emerson Middle School targeted for closure (Grannan, 2010). Emerson Middle School was spared.

Along with segregated charter schools, segregated traditional public schools also can be found. Unlike Emerson, little attempt has been made to integrate students based on racial school assignments in recent years.

In 2007, *Parents Involved in Community Schools v. Seattle School District No. 1* and *Meredith v. Jefferson County Board of Education* sought and succeeded not to allow race to dominate student placement. The bitterly divided Supreme Court dealt a blow to diversity plans when they voted 5–4 that race could not be a factor in public school student assignments. This decision continues to threaten integration plans in school districts across the country.

## SPECIAL EDUCATION

If Americans want a preview of school privatization and the rejection of students with disabilities, they need only look to New Orleans. No one disputes New Orleans public schools were in desperate condition before Katrina. But in 2007, Naomi Klein's *The Shock Doctrine* describes how Milton Friedman and political friends, backed by "tens of millions of dollars" from the Bush administration, used Katrina's devastation to privatize New Orleans public schools.[18]

In 2010, Education Secretary Arne Duncan said in an interview:

> I spent a lot of time in New Orleans, and this is a tough thing to say, but let me be really honest. I think the best thing that happened to the education system in New Orleans was Hurricane Katrina. That education system was a disaster, and it took Hurricane Katrina to wake up the community to say that "we have to do better." And the progress that they've made in four years since the hurricane is unbelievable.[19]

Duncan should have added that Katrina also blew away years of progress made to serve and protect the educational interests of disadvantaged children and students with disabilities. New Orleans charter schools rejected students with disabilities, and a complaint filed in 2009 alleged some New Orleans charter schools also discriminated against African American students.

A meeting, hosted by the federal education department's Office of Civil Rights with 150 state and local administrators, was held to discuss federal laws that protect students (Reckdahl, 2010). Charter schools had no funds to provide special education services, and the regional compliance team leader, John Stephens, appeared puzzled over the audience's concerns when asked questions about charter school structure relating to these populations.

Regular public schools typically have built-in support, including district and school specialists, psychologists, speech pathologists, social workers, counselors, and special educators. School districts include special education directors who consult and assist school principals in order to ensure that the rights of students with disabilities are met.

Most charter schools have no such staff of experts. Still, special education is supposed to be governed by federal and state rules and regulations in order to protect the rights of children with disabilities, and, when charter schools do not enforce those laws, it would appear that they are breaking the law.

In 2001, the National Association of State Directors of Special Education studied how various state charter schools interpreted special education laws and regulations (Ahearn, 2001). They found little continuity of services. Roles and responsibilities were ill-defined. Charter school applications and contracts provided little guarantee of special education provisions. No follow-up procedures took place to ensure services were being provided.

Many charter school operators have little understanding of federal/state/local special education funding sources and have difficulty hiring prepared special education staff, teachers, and related services personnel. Most charter schools teach everyone the same material and do not subscribe to individualized special education requirements. Students either understand the scripted program and the assignments or they leave the school.

A number of legal issues surround denied services for students with disabilities in charter schools. In Palm Beach County, the Florida State Conference of the NAACP, the Southern Legal Aid Society of Palm Beach County, and the Southern Poverty Law Center filed complaints regarding students diagnosed with behavioral or emotional disabilities not getting the required services they need (Bridges4Kids).

The Southern Poverty Law Center represented students with disabilities in New Orleans who did not have access to special education due to the charter school system. In 2011, a federal judge denied the Louisiana Department of Education's motion to dismiss a lawsuit on behalf of these students. In 2014, the Education Department, school board, and law center announced they had reached a settlement for students with disabilities and charter schools.

The State of Louisiana was to create a plan to track charter schools to ensure school progress, guarantee student identification and evaluation, provide student services, and safeguard adequate plans. The state and school board would review discipline policies and provide assistance. Schools would have to describe how they check on discrimination regarding students with disabilities (Dreilinger, 2014). Concerns surfaced as to who would pay for the lawsuit, and many worry still whether students with disabilities will be adequately served in New Orleans.

## KIPP

A variety of chain charter schools are operated in America, but the best known is KIPP (Knowledge Is Power Program). At this time, ninety KIPP middle schools (grades five through eight), seventy-one elementary schools (grades prekindergarten to four), and twenty-two high schools (grades nine through twelve) can be found mostly in urban areas. KIPP's website is a marketing blitz. They currently display complimentary media reports and have promoted their schools on major networks. They have KIPP videos. A *USA Today* editorial cheering KIPP said "the improbable idea that urban schools can succeed now seems thinkable."[20]

Well-known celebrities such as Oprah Winfrey and Bill Gates have promoted KIPP. Dave Levin and Mike Feinberg, from Teach for America, are cofounders of KIPP, along with the late Gap founder Donald Fisher. Fisher's involvement with KIPP originally drew suspicion since he had strong ties to Chris Whittle's failed for-profit Edison Schools (Walsh, 2001). After his death, son John Fisher became his replacement on the KIPP Board of Directors along with Doris Fisher, Donald Fisher's wife.

KIPP CEO Richard Barth is married to Wendy Kopp, founder of Teach for America (TFA). Barth managed Chris Whittle's Edison Schools before going to work at KIPP. He is on the founding TFA staff, is an Aspen Institute-New Schools Fellow, and sits on the board of directors of the Broad Center for the Management of School Systems and Be the Change, Inc. Barth's BA is in American History from Harvard University. Like his wife, he has no background in education or experience working with children.

KIPP has five pillars to live by, which include:

- High Expectations
- Choice and Commitment
- More Time
- Power to Lead
- Focus on Results[21]

KIPP is full of platitudes, the favorites being "Work Hard. Be Nice" and "Knowledge Is Power" (acronym for title). But all is not rosy at KIPP. A

2011 Western Michigan University study determined KIPP to have a high level of attrition (Miron, Urschel, and Saxton, 2011). And KIPP-funded students, through public and private financing, are funded at a rate of $6,500 more than public school students. Cost per student at KIPP was listed from $4,200 to $17,200, depending on the community (KIPP, 2014). When KIPP dismisses students who have challenging behavior problems, including second-language students, those students return to traditional public schools. This all raises questions as to whether schools like KIPP could ever fully replace public schools.

Serious concerns have been raised about KIPP's cultlike discipline—isolation and shunning. It is well documented that students usually "have to write letters of apology for even minor infractions—being late, say, or forgetting to wear the complete uniform. At some schools, miscreants have to sit on a bench wearing a sign that says 'Bench.'"[22] Merriam-Webster's online dictionary defines *miscreant* as "infidel or heretic," as "one who behaves criminally or viciously."[23]

Multiple problems concerning troubling disciplinary practices at a KIPP Academy Fresno Charter School surfaced in 2008 and were present as early as 2004 after KIPP opened there (Dudley, Ginis, and Ginis, 2009). Concerns about discipline issues caused some parents to remove their children in 2009 from the KIPP South Fulton Academy near Atlanta (Vogell, 2009).

Kipsters march in order, recite lessons, and chant responses in military-like fashion. Students are reprimanded when they misspeak or misdirect their gazes from speakers. Incidences where children sit in the corner with a dunce cap have been reported. In 2013, two KIPP students, a kindergartner and first-grader, were punished by being placed in a padded room (Monahan and Chapman, 2013).

KIPP students can lose their desks as punishment, or they may be forced to earn a desk (Horn, 2013). Many KIPP students sit on the floor to work or listen to the teacher. But while questions surrounding KIPP's troubling disciplinary practices might create controversy in the news one day, it seems soon forgotten.

Many overlook such displays of punishment. There are those who believe such tactics are necessary, even creative, to reign in poor, inner-city students. Yet no justification exists for such sternness. It is suggested that traditional public schools be more like KIPP. But public schools rarely work the way KIPP works—why should they? It could be argued that KIPP displays low expectations of students.

KIPP students are not always thrilled with having to attend the charter school. Leonie Haimson, founder of Class Size Matters, in a post on Schools Matter interviewed a former KIPP student. She writes how students call KIPP the "Kids in Prison Program," and how the penal pedagogy found at the school "represents the second coming of Eugenics."[24]

Yet some consider KIPP creators, Feinberg and Levin, the go-to guys to teach public school teachers and principals how to run schools, even though they come from Teach for America. Hunter College of Education, the largest college in the City University of New York (CUNY) system, announced a pro-charter-school partnership with Achievement First, KIPP, Uncommon Schools, and the New York City Charter School Center to create a teacher preparation program called Relay Graduate School of Education. But there has been no proof the program creates better teachers. Teachers watch online videos.

Relay is setting up near universities across the country. In 2014, it was announced they would be working within the University of Memphis, recruiting college students from other academic areas to become fast-track teachers. They were to work alongside the College of Education. Parents, teachers, and professors protested, and the group set up shop outside of the university.

## CONCLUSION: THE END OF CHARTER SCHOOLS

In communities across the country, politicians and business leaders refuse to appropriately fund public schools, closing them and reopening charter schools run by a variety of nonprofit or for-profit charter school management groups. Parents, unhappy about poor schools, have welcomed charter schools into their communities. But that looks to be changing.

School closures cause problems for students and their families. They sometimes live far from the charter school, creating transportation difficulties. In the city, teenagers might be placed in rival schools, provoking gang confrontations. Qualified teachers are often let go when schools close. When charter schools are opened in their place, it is unlikely veteran teachers will get their positions back. If they do, they probably will no longer get health insurance and benefits. Some teachers refuse to work in charter schools.

What started out as a way to give teachers autonomy and a creative voice has become a movement to dismantle public schooling. Instead of serving *all children*, charter schools separate and divide the kinds of students they select, raising questions about democratic governance and the future of our children and the country.

And the tide might be turning when it comes to charter school popularity. More and more, citizens are learning about scandals surrounding charter schools in their states. Websites such as Charter School Scandals by Sharon Higgins inform the public of problematic charter schools. And social media and bloggers are writing critical reviews about charter schools more than ever before. Parents and educators are becoming better informed about charter school problems, and they are organizing to stop them from opening. Many parents want more charter school transparency.

In 2015, the Center for Popular Democracy and the Alliance to Reclaim Our Schools described the cost in fraud and mismanagement of charter school funding in fifteen states to add up to over $200 million. Fears that local governments stood to eventually lose more than $1.4 billion in 2015 was mentioned in the report.

Along with this, in states and communities across the country, parents, teachers, and citizens are uniting to find ways to support public schools. Parents Across America is a group with state chapters and affiliates addressing school concerns. Save Our Schools is another organization bringing education activists together. They gained recognition in 2011 for a well-attended march in Washington, DC.

In 2013, Chicago Public Schools closed 54 of 129 public schools originally considered for closure. Some 7,000 parents, teachers, and students protested for three days (Kelly, 2015). And a dozen activists who wanted to keep Dyett High School open in the South Side went on a hunger strike that lasted thirty-four days (Perez, 2015). CPS said Dyett was to reopen as an arts school. While the hunger strikers did not get what they requested, many sympathized with their activism.

In Milwaukee, Wisconsin, parents, teachers, and students protested the education budget put forth by Gov. Scott Walker because it included cuts that would harm public schools (Ollstein, 2015). Many now reject public school privatization there.

In 2015, Washington State's Supreme Court got to the heart of the charter/public school debate, calling charters "unconstitutional" because they don't have an elected school board and are not accountable to the voters.[25] This sends a message to citizens in Washington and other states to reconsider the differences between charter schools and public schools.

Many parents speak out at local school board meetings—like in Boston, where parents fought hard to keep traditional public schools open, or New Jersey, where one parent took it upon herself to research and try to stop a religiously ill-defined charter school from opening (Horn, 2012). While these attempts may not always succeed, they are steps in the right direction. The era of charter schools looks to be on the decline.

## NOTES

1. American Federation of Teachers, Charter Schools, http://www.aftacts.org/about-us/aft-and-charter-schools.
2. Hillary Clinton, remarks made to the National Education Association (NEA) in Orlando, Florida, July 5, 1999.
3. "Get the Facts," National Alliance for Public Charter Schools, http://www.publiccharters.org/get-the-facts/public-charter-schools/faqs/.
4. Kent Fischer, "Public School Inc.," *St. Petersburg Times*, September 15, 2002.
5. Vicki McClure and Mary Shanklin, "Charter Schools: Missing the Grade. Parts 1–4," *Orlando Sentinel*, March 26, 2007.
6. Foundation for Excellence, http://excelined.org/.
7. Jennifer Dixon, "Michigan Spends $1 Billion on Charter Schools But Fails to Hold Them Accountable," *Detroit Free Press*, June 22, 2014.
8. Michael Dobbs, "Charter vs. Traditional: Two Types of D.C. Public School Are Not Easy to Compare," *Washington Post*, December 15, 2000.
9. Caroline Hoxby, "A Serious Statistical Mistake in the CREDO Study of Charter Schools," Stanford University and NBER, August 2009, http://credo.stanford.edu/reports/memo_on_the_credo_study.pdf.
10. CREDO, "Fact vs. Fiction: An Analysis of Dr. Hoxby's Misrepresentation of CREDO's Research," Stanford University, October 7, 2009, http://credo.stanford.edu/reports/CREDO_Hoxby_Rebuttal.pdf.
11. Gerald Bracey, "The Washington Post—Union Buster?" *Huffington Post*, November 30, 2009, www.huffingtonpost.com/gerald-bracey/the-washington-post--unio_b_305238.html.
12. Martin Carnoy, Rebecca Jacobsen, Lawrence Mishel, and Richard Rothstein, *The Charter School Dust-Up* (Washington, DC: Teachers College Press and Economic Policy Institute, 2005), 126.
13. Erica Frankenberg, Genevieve Siegel-Hawley, and Jia Wang, *Choice without Equity: Charter School Segregation and the Need for Civil Rights Standards* (Los Angeles, CA: The Civil Rights Project/Proyecto Derechos Civiles at UCLA, January 2010), http://civilrightsproject.ucla.edu/research/k-12-education/integration-and-diversity/choice-without-equity-2009-report.
14. Ibid.
15. Susan Ohanian, "New Yorker Profile of Charter School Chief Steve Barr Is Propaganda, not Reporting," *Substance News*, May 26, 2009.
16. Douglas McGray, "The Instigator," *The New Yorker*, May 11, 2009, http://newamerica.net/node/9335.
17. Carolyn Jacobson, "LAUSD, Green Dot and the Voice of a Teacher," Schools Matter, September 30, 2009, http://www.schoolsmatter.info/search?q=emerson+middle+school.

18. Naomi Klein, *The Shock Doctrine* (New York: Picador, 2007), 5–7.

19. Nick Anderson, "Education Secretary Duncan Calls Hurricane Katrina Good for New Orleans Schools," *Washington Post*, January 30, 2010.

20. "An Urban Success Story," Editorial, *USA Today*, October 3, 2005.

21. KIPP, Five Pillars, http://www.kipp.org/our-approach/five-pillars.

22. Nanette Asimov, "Students at KIPP Perform Better, Study Finds," *San Francisco Chronicle*, September 18, 2008.

23. Merriam-Webster's Online Dictionary, http://www.merriam-webster.com/dictionary/miscreants.

24. Leonie Haimson, "Why Students Call KIPP the Kids in Prison Program," Schools Matter, March 23, 2012, http://www.schoolsmatter.info/.

25. Emma Brown, "What Makes a Public School Public? Washington State Court Finds Charter Schools Unconstitutional," *Washington Post*, September 9, 2015.

# *Chapter Three*

# Students, Jobs, and the Global Economy

> Find what it is that interests you and that you can do well, and when you find it, put your whole soul into it.
>
> —John D. Rockefeller III

## SCAPEGOATS

Throughout the 1980s, the Japanese school success story provided critics of US public schools part of the basis for the critical report *A Nation at Risk*. By the 1990s, talk of Japan's schools mysteriously disappeared. Why?

In 2006, the late educational researcher Gerald Bracey explained the problems that can occur when attempting to associate economies to student test scores. "Japan's 'bubble burst' even though students still aced their tests. In America, students continued to score in the middle of the pack, but the economy boomed and the World Economic Forum ranked us No. 1 in global competitiveness among over 100 nations."[1]

During the Clinton administration, when the economy flourished, America's public school students still, to borrow a phrase from the late Rodney Dangerfield, "got no respect." Instead, America witnessed a push for standards, high-stakes testing, school uniforms, character education, zero tolerance, and charter schools.

Little seemed learned from Japan's lesson. Politicians and many businessmen blamed, and continue to condemn, public schools for not being able to find well-prepared workers for their companies. But the economic problems we face are not caused by public schools. American students are being used as scapegoats.

Free trade supporter and Princeton University economics professor Alan S. Blinder voiced concerns in 2007 about outsourcing America's jobs overseas. Blinder estimated thirty to forty million US jobs could be outsourced. Those threatened included scientists, mathematicians, editors, telephone operators, clerks, and typists. But Blinder did not blame public schools for this economic shift. Instead, he acknowledged that "bosses" would turn to overseas workers who would "happily work for a fraction of what Americans earn."[2]

Richard Rothstein, former *New York Times* reporter and research associate with the Economic Policy Institute, blames the popularization of negative thinking about public schools on books and organizations. He points to Thomas Friedman's *The World Is Flat*, the Bill and Melinda Gates Foundation, and other foundations and groups such as the Alliance for Excellent Education.

He writes, "Over the last few decades, wages of college graduates overall have increased, but some—managers, executives, white-collar sales workers—have commandeered disproportionate shares of national productivity gains, with little left over for scientists, engineers, teachers, programmers and others with high levels of skill. No amount of school reform can undo tax, regulatory and labor market policies that redirect wealth generated by skilled workers to profits and executive bonuses."[3] Rothstein refers to a report blaming schools called "Tough Choices or Tough Times" by Marc Tucker.

## STANDARDS

> The fact is that education holds the key to personal and national economic well-being, more now than at any time in our history.
>
> —Marc Tucker[4]

Marc Tucker propelled himself onto the education scene in the 1980s, rising to prominence and power. Despite no economics or education degree, he helped author the Carnegie report *A Nation Prepared: Teachers for the 21st Century*, which followed *A Nation at Risk.* Here is how Tucker is described by the National Center on Education and the Economy, an organization he founded:

> Marc has been a leader of the standards-driven education reform movement for many years. Mr. Tucker created New Standards, a 23-state consortium designed to develop internationally benchmarked student performance standards and matching student examinations. He authored the 1986 Carnegie Report, *A Nation Prepared: Teachers for the 21st Century*, which called for a restructuring of America's schools based on standards; created the National Board for Professional Teaching Standards; created the Commission on the Skills of the American Workforce and co-authored its report, *America's Choice: High Skills or Low Wages!*, which called for a new high school leaving a certificate based on standards; and, was instrumental in creating the National Skill Standards Board and served as the chairman of its committee on standards and assessment policy.
>
> With Ray Marshall, Mr. Tucker co-authored *Thinking for a Living: Education and the Wealth of Nations*, selected by *Business Week* as one of the ten best business books of 1992; with Judy Codding, co-authored *Standards for Our Schools: How to Set Them, Measure Them, and Reach Them*, published in 1998; and co-edited *The Principal Challenge*, 2002. Mr. Tucker created the National Institute of School Leadership, a state-of-the-art executive development program for school leaders. Mr. Tucker was the lead author of *Tough Choices or Tough Times*, the report of the New Commission on the Skills of the American Workforce. In 2014, the Education Commission of the States awarded Mr. Tucker the James Bryant Conant award for his outstanding individual contribution to American education. Mr. Tucker currently has an appointment as a Visiting Distinguished Fellow at the Harvard Graduate School of Education.[5]

Tucker initially criticized teachers and public schools, and his initiatives paved the way for school privatization (Carnegie Corporation of New York, 1986). The non-peer-reviewed, 168-page thesis alleged that fewer well-educated teachers were employed, that teachers should receive bachelor degrees in arts and sciences and master's degrees in teaching, and that teacher compensation should be like other careers—competitive with incentives. While teachers often sought to better their education by acquiring master's degrees, the report made it sound as if this was a new idea.

Tucker's plan also introduced the role of lead teacher and the National Board Certification Program emphasizing National Board Standards for teachers. Both initiatives perpetuated the idea that teachers were ill-prepared to teach and needed further assistance and/or proof of their ability.

The Pew Charitable Trusts and the John D. and Catherine T. MacArthur Foundation funded a large part of the New Standards Project. In 1989 Tucker established the National Center on Education and the Economy (NCEE), not to be confused with the National Council on Economic Education. The NCEE secured a troupe of nationally known figures, including the director of the University of Pittsburgh's Learning Research and Development Center Lauren Resnick (Viadero, 1994). They created the report *America's Choice: High Skills or Low Wages*. Resnick sat on the Common Core State Standards Initiative Validation Committee.

Along with Tucker's work, in 1991, the Department of Labor produced the report SCANS, defining what American workers should know for the global economy. Large in scope, the report alarmed educators and parents who believed it allotted too much power to the federal government to control and reorganize education.

In 1992, Ira C. Magaziner and Hillary Rodham Clinton cowrote "Will America Choose High Skills or Low Wages?" published in *Educational Leadership*. The report blamed declining American competitiveness in the world economy on decreased worker productivity, lacking school performance standards, and poor student motivation (1992).

Also, in 1992, Marc Tucker's "Dear Hillary [Clinton] Letter" had the same theme. The letter appears to outline a restructuring plan that involves predetermined jobs for children (Schaffer, 1998). In 1994, President Clinton signed Goals 2000, the School-to-Work Opportunities Act, and the Improving America's Schools Act. Later, Tucker's ideas figured prominently in the formulation of No Child Left Behind.

The conservative Eagle Forum outlined Tucker's letter as "ambitious," describing how his plans were implemented in three laws passed by Congress. The Forum outlines three goals relative to restructuring public schools outlined in the Dear Hillary letter:

1. Bypass all elected officials on school boards and in state legislatures by making federal funds flow to the governor and his appointees on workforce development boards.
2. Use a computer database, aka "a labor market information system," into which school personnel would scan all information about every schoolchild and his family, identified by the child's social security number: academic, medical, mental, psychological, behavioral, and interrogations by counselors. The computerized data would be available to the school, the government, and future employers.
3. Use "national standards" and "national testing" to cement national control of tests, assessments, school honors and rewards, financial aid,

and the Certificate of Initial Mastery (CIM), which is designed to replace the high school diploma.[6]

Conservative spokesperson Phyllis Schlafly claimed Tucker "has re-emerged to sell us old wine in new bottles."[7] School systems, she insisted, would focus on "minimum competencies. Students will be pigeon-holed into jobs to serve the best interests of the local economy as decided by the bureaucrats, not into careers chosen by the student."[8]

In 2007, the NCEE published "Tough Choices or Tough Times," funded by the Bill and Melinda Gates Foundation. The report, with the help of the New Commission on the Skills of the American Workforce, asserts that higher education is the answer to economic well-being, but that well-educated Americans are at risk for outsourcing due to the failure of public schools. The report notes, "What is essential is that we create a seamless web of opportunities, to develop one's skills that literally extends from cradle to grave and is the same system for everyone—young and old, poor and rich, worker and full-time student."

Economist and president of the Economic Policy Institute Lawrence Mishel and writer Richard Rothstein criticized what they viewed "as erroneous assertions and unsound recommendations from the 'Tough Choices Tough Times' report." This includes:

1. The assumption that schools are the only factor necessary for a good economy and that "the past decade's productivity surge" has nothing to do with the success of recent graduates.
2. The idea that higher productivity will lead to higher living standards and equitable distribution of wealth (not happening).
3. That teacher quality will improve with higher pay by abolishing defined benefits and creating a private employee teacher retirement system.
4. The negative views that teachers are less able than those in other professions. This is a myth.
5. That the dropout situation is as bad as we are told, calling the claims "wildly exaggerated."
6. That school districts should be abolished in favor of contracts between private providers and school districts.[9]

At this time, the *Chronicle of Higher Education* reported that the New Commission on the Skills of the American Workforce, a panel of political, business, and higher-education leaders, had laid out "a sweeping proposal for overhauling the nation's education system."[10] In the same report, Tucker complains that public school changes, enacted by the federal government and the states, had not produced output.

America's Choice, a for-profit subsidiary of the NCEE, along with the University of Pennsylvania, contracted with school districts to evaluate schools, charging $70,000 for elementary schools and $75,000 for high schools (Toch, 2005). NCEE played an intricate role in Race to the Top and Common Core State Standards. In 2010, America's Choice was purchased for $80 million by Pearson PLC (Gewertz, 2010).

Also, in 2010, in a *Phi Delta Kappan* article "Tying Together the Common Core of Standards, Instruction, and Assessments," Vicki Phillips and Carina Wong, both working for the Bill and Melinda Gates Foundation, promote the work they did on the standards and their earlier association to the NCEE and the New Standards Project in the 1990s. In the article, they state:

> The vision of a sensible and challenging education for all students has always been central to this work, but when we were dealing with states and school districts, we often stumbled at trying to move systems. There were too many pieces to change at the same time, and never enough money and a lack of political stamina at all levels. The No Child Left Behind Act helped set priorities, but the prescriptive accountability measures made it difficult for some districts and states to use assessments as levers for good practices.
>
> With the Common Core of Standards, many things now become possible.[11]

In 2015, Tucker, blogging for *Education Week*, said that civil rights groups should reconsider testing:

> Those who argue that annual accountability testing of every child is essential for the advancement of poor and minority children ought to be able to show that poor and minority children perform better in education systems that have such requirements and worse in systems that don't have them. But that is simply not the case. Many nations that have no annual accountability testing requirements have higher average performance for poor and minority students and smaller gaps between their performance and the performance of majority students than we do here in the United States. How can annual testing be a civil right if that is so?[12]

## COLLEGE FOR ALL

> There has been a dramatic drop in demand for workers with even the highest levels of education.
>
> —*The State of Working America*[13]

Tucker and those with similar ideology blame public schools for a poor economy and believe problems will be solved if everyone attends college. But in 2007, writer Barbara Ehrenreich likely stunned graduating seniors at prestigious Haverford College with her commencement speech titled "The Apocalypse Is Yours Now." Ehrenreich said:

> At the moment you accept your diploma today, you will have an average debt of $20,000 and no health insurance. You may be feeling desperate enough to take whatever comes along. Some of you will get caged in cubicles until you're ejected by the next wave of layoffs. Others—some of the best and brightest of you in fact—will still be behind a counter in Starbucks or Borders three years down the road. Parents, if that happens to your child, don't blame him or her, because the sad fact is that the middle class is crumbling under our feet just as these accomplished young people are setting out to find a place in it—destroyed by layoffs and outsourcings and by severe under-funding for vital fields like science, social work, and education. Benefits are evaporating, and job security is a thing of the past.[14]

Ehrenreich's speech included more sad tidbits about war, the environment, and the economy, leaving a commenter to sum up the speech on Ehrenreich's blog with "Congratulations, kids . . . YOU'RE [Expletive]!" Others blamed Ehrenreich for being too negative. Yet despite the uncertainty, Ehrenreich noted that the "college for everyone" mantra continues to be promoted.

It is true that college graduates make more money than their non-college-educated peers, but fewer jobs exist for their employment, and students are graduating deeply in debt. In 2008, Paul E. Barton, education writer, consultant, and senior associate in the Policy Information Center at the Educational Testing Service, authored an article for *Change* magazine asking, "How many college graduates does the U.S. labor force need?" He states, "Compelling evidence does not exist that there will be a rapid rise in the general demand for college graduates and a damaging shortfall in their supply sufficient to cause the United States to falter in the world economy."[15]

The US Department of Labor's 2012 projections included more jobs in service, and some jobs only require high school diplomas. One area in high demand includes personal and home care aides to assist aging baby boomers. Elderly care involves individuals with understanding and compassion more than competitive degrees. Assistants in fields such as physical and occupational therapy were also needed.

Echoing Ehrenreich and Barton's predictions, in 2014, a report by the Economic Policy Institute indicated the US labor market continued to be rough on young workers, and job prospects for college graduates had improved little (Shierholz, Davis, and Kimball, 2014).

## PRIVATIZED HIGH SCHOOL PROGRAMS

Will Advanced Placement (AP) make a better, more employable student? AP used to mean an occasional college credit class for a motivated student who excelled. Now AP is big business and a privatized approach to schooling. One must ask why students cannot take advanced classes without the College Board. The College Board makes a profit on fees for teacher training, AP exams, and books sold for exam review. It currently costs $87 per AP test, but that is always subject to change.

AP classes push students to cover material at a faster rate in order to pass tests that ensure college credit, hence the term *advanced*, or sometimes classes are called *accelerated*. Being in AP, however, fails to adequately address the unique needs of gifted and/or talented students (Dixon, 2006). AP classes can be monotonous and stressful, and they have been criticized for being standardized and focused on high-stakes test taking. The benefit of AP is that students might be able to skip some college classes—many colleges permit this. Even if colleges do not give course credit, the more AP classes taken the better a student ranks in high school. This improves the chances of being accepted into college. Parents spend thousands of dollars per year (depending on how many children they have) paying for advanced classes, preparation booklets, and repeat testing.

Some school waivers are provided to those who cannot afford AP exams, but AP often caters to wealthy students. Wealthy schools have more AP classes than poor schools. Even if students from lower socioeconomic households take AP courses, it is not guaranteed they will go to college. Poor students require more financial aid, which may not be available.

Next to AP, International Baccalaureate (IB) is considered the king of school programs. Both continuously jockey to be best. M. Blouke Carus, a publisher who felt a need existed for American students to be competitive with their counterparts around the world, introduced the Geneva, Switzerland–based IB program to this country. IB started overseas in schools for the children of diplomats.

The overall cost per school for the IB program depends on a number of choices school officials make (International Baccalaureate Organization). A website called Truth About IB says program preparation costs $1,500 per teacher, and the school application fee is $23,000 per school, along with a variety of other costs. Online teacher preparation is approximately $620 per teacher per six-week course. It is unclear what the overall cost is for parents.

*Newsweek*'s Best High Schools frequently include those with IB status. Some parents, however, worry that IB destroys American values and a student's ability to learn American culture, especially in the area of literature. IB focuses more on international books. It is also more project oriented compared to AP.

Whatever parents think of AP and IB, these programs influence what students learn. They introduce a for-profit element to public schooling, and the emphasis on passing a test at the culmination of the class impacts how classes are taught. Students who do not participate in AP or IB may find themselves segregated in regular classes considered less rigorous.

## STEM

> To train our workers for the jobs of tomorrow, we've made education reform a top priority in this administration. We are not interested in just putting more money into our schools; we want that money moving toward reform. And last year we launched a national competition to improve our schools based on a simple idea: Instead of funding the status quo, we will only invest in reform—reform that raises student achievement and inspires students to excel in math and science, and turns around failing schools that steal the future of too many young Americans. I just met this week with the nation's governors, and education reform is one of those rare issues where both Democrats and Republicans are enthusiastic.
>
> —President Barack Obama[16]

Take chances, make mistakes, get messy!
—Ms. Frizzle on *The Magic School Bus*

In 2010, Sally Ride, one of America's favorite astronauts, appeared on CNN plugging Change the Equation (CTE) for STEM—science, technology, engineering, and math. Ride said, "I think that for the last 20, 25 years, our society really hasn't put a focus on the importance of science and math education."[17] Echoing rhetoric from other reformers, Ride also said "80 percent of the jobs over the next decade are going to require some background, some basic skills in science and math. So even for the students in school today to grow up and have living wage jobs, they need this background."[18]

Ride's effort to interest girls in science and math careers with science camps was a commendable goal. A national dialogue about public schooling and women in STEM careers is always welcome. But the anxiety-laden rhetoric about STEM jobs presented by Ride, President Obama, Bill Gates, and others is overplayed and unnecessarily critical of public schools. The high emphasis for increased STEM seems more about privatized for-profit programs and a means to vilify public schools.

The media often implies that students drop out of STEM coursework in college because of course difficulty. This further condemns public schools. But most evidence shows it is not that students find science too difficult in college. Students leave science majors when they realize little hope exists of finding a well-paying job in science!

Numerous reports prove this point. In 2009, *USA Today*'s "Scientist Shortage? Maybe Not" describes a RAND National Defense Research Institute study that finds no shortages in science and challenges the National Science Foundation for their claim of an increased need for scientists (Toppo and Vergano, 2009).

In 2010, *Scientific American* asked, "Does the U.S. Produce Too Many Scientists?" They insist the real problem is a lack of available quality career opportunities for the many talented scientists who graduate from America's universities every year (Benderly, 2010). A better question would be, What great discoveries are lost to the world because scientists cannot find science jobs?

Important questions have also arisen about the cost of hiring qualified scientists in science posts. Even with a shortage of science positions, senators Chuck Schumer (D-NY) and John Cornyn (R-TX) promoted, in 2012, and again in 2013, a push to give green cards to foreign students with STEM degrees to work in America.

Serious gaps, however, do exist in public school STEM instruction. Quality programs are more difficult to find in low-income areas. Disparities are created through insufficient funding of public schools and by not making STEM a priority in the school curriculum.

For example, the new Common Core State Standards (CCSS) emphasize reading and math—not science, although Next Generation Science is being developed. But what kind of science instruction are students receiving today? The math standards for CCSS are also controversial due to confusion surrounding lessons. Standards in general have driven science exploration out of the classroom.

A narrowing of the curriculum and the reality of shoddy science instruction is ignored by most who seek to reform schools. In 2007, a Congressional Subcommittee met to discuss serious issues surrounding science instruction in public schools. They found a "lack of coordination between the laboratory exercises and classroom lectures, inadequately trained teachers, languishing facilities, and poor high school organization."[19]

Government incentives do not adequately address these issues. They include groups such as Change the Equation, which funds specific private, for-profit programs meant to improve science instruction; the College Board's Advanced Placement Training and Incentive Program; the Museum of Boston's Engineering is Elementary; FIRST Robotics; Intel Math from the University of Vermont; Sally Ride Science; New York Hall of Science's Science Career Ladder; and the UTeach STEM (advertised as a "shorter, cheaper path to certification") program from the University of Texas (Change the Equation).

While there may be worth in these programs, they are heavily marketed by negatively portraying America's public schools as losing their competitive edge. They also do not tackle the instructional needs in public school STEM classes. They are pricey programs, and not everyone has access.

Ironically, America could be in danger of diminishing STEM positions in this country due to the real lack of STEM investment in public schools. Upgrading science labs and incorporating more hands-on lab STEM instruction is needed. Introducing young children to the joy of science in a way as to foster interest is also important.

Also, what does STEM really mean? When corporate CEOs complain today about not having enough STEM workers, or talent, they are often referring to STEM careers that are more about career-technical training.

While public schools should offer quality STEM programs, many concerns surround Common Core State Standards in math and the Next Generation Science Standards. The Thomas Fordham Institute gives ratings to the science standards, but they are a conservative think tank, and their ratings vary according to states. The overall question is, Why should America rely on science standards, or any standards, created by an elite group? Science was well addressed in public schools in the past, but until better programs are introduced, teachers should continue to teach science with what they know.

## VOCATIONAL—CAREER AND TECHNICAL EDUCATION

Vocational education, often called Career and Technical Education (CTE), appears to be making a revival in public schools. In Tucson, Arizona, a Joint Technical Education program involved a ramped-up metals shop that incorporates technology and troubleshoots automotive difficulties (Axelson, 2009).

In Canton, Massachusetts, the Blue Hills Regional Technical High School focuses on technology along with metal work, carpentry, and HVAC—modernized when compared with past instruction. And at San Diego's Kearny High School, four specialized programs dominate their CTE program involving science and technology and digital media along with design.

According to a 2014 report, the US Department of Labor, Bureau of Labor Statistics, the following positions call for a high school diploma, or the equivalent, and possibly moderate-term or long-term on-the-job training (a few call for an apprenticeship):

- Automotive body and related repairers
- Bookkeeping, accounting, and auditing clerks
- Bus drivers, transit and intercity
- Computer-controlled machine tool operators, metal and plastic
- Construction and building inspectors
- Crane and tower operators
- Eligibility interviewers, government programs
- Excavating and loading machine and dragline operators
- Glaziers

- Hazardous materials removal workers
- Industrial machinery mechanics
- Insurance sales agents
- Maintenance workers, machinery
- Millwrights
- Mobile heavy equipment mechanics, except engines
- Occupational Health and Safety technicians
- Operating engineers and other construction equipment operators
- Painters, transportation equipment
- Payroll and timekeeping clerks
- Private detectives and investigators
- Property, real estate, and community association managers
- Real estate sales agents
- Sheet metal workers
- Surveying and mapping technicians

Vocational education has changed throughout the years. The Smith-Hughes National Vocational Education Act of 1917 provided students with agricultural skills. Later, the Act focused on national defense and community colleges. The Vocational Education Act of 1963 was designed to provide training for students not going on to college, and it played a vital role in preparing young people with skills for employment after high school. Federal funds were authorized to support research in vocation education, vocational work-study programs, and business education.

Representative Carl Dewey Perkins from Kentucky championed education and President Johnson's war on poverty. He rallied behind programs such as Head Start, school lunches, adult education, libraries, and federal aid for the poor in the depressed Appalachian region. But he is best known for his support of vocational education.

In 1984, under President H. W. Bush, the Carl D. Perkins Vocational Education Act included important changes for students. It improved access to underserved students and those with disabilities and limited English proficiency. It amended the 1968 and 1976 Act, stipulating that funds be used for high school, postsecondary students, and students who were completing, or who left, high school and required retraining in the labor market (Gordon, 2008, 94). Vocational school facilities, vocational guidance, and training and ancillary services, such as program evaluations, became a priority.

In 2006, the George W. Bush administration reauthorized the Carl D. Perkins Vocational and Technical Education Act amid fears that it would be eliminated. The reauthorization included changes to special education law. Vocational and technical training became standardized like other subjects, with less emphasis on individualized training for non-college-bound students (2006). The new Act also made state grants harder to obtain for students with difficulties in core classes. The changes went a long way to destroy the premise of the original amendment.

Although the initial Perkins Act placed students into well-paying, working-class positions and provided training for non-college-bound students, some believed it pigeonholed students into a noncollege track, and that such a track was substandard. Minority students appeared to be placed more often in vocational education while wealthy students took college preparatory classes. This led to the notion that public schools failed minority students.

For years, vocational education seemed pushed aside—even scorned—but renamed Career and Technical Education (CTE), it is making a comeback. The US Department of Education claims that enrollment for these programs has increased to 57 percent, from 9.6 million students in 1999 to 15.1 million in 2004 (Vail, 2007). High schools should offer a variety CTE classes, and students should be permitted to obtain crossover credit in both vocational and college preparation classes.

Concerns involve career-technical training and school-to-work opportunities. Students who wish to bypass college may obtain valuable on-the-job training for possible careers after high school graduation. The question is, How young is too young for students to decide what careers they want to pursue in the future? Should high school be about college preparation?

Whether students choose to attend college or work in vocational-technical careers, the decision might better be made through academic and career counseling and student interest and desire. High school students should not be directed into programs that fit the need of outside corporations. High school is a time for students to learn about their career interests.

In 2013, President Obama visited Pathways in Technology Early College High School (P-Tech), where he hailed the school for preparing students with skills for the workforce. He said, "In previous generations, America's standing economically was so much higher than everybody else's that we didn't have a lot of competition. Now, you've got billions of people from Beijing to Bangalore to Moscow, all of whom are competing with you directly. And they're—those countries are working every day, to out-educate and outcompete us."[20]

But schools like P-Tech raise questions about whether high school students are developmentally ready to choose a career, and how much involvement in high schools should corporate partnerships play? P-Tech involves collaborate agreements with Microsoft, Motorola, and Verizon.[21] The fear is that young people might be steered into a predetermined school coursework that will benefit corporations.

In *The Shame of the Nation: The Restoration of Apartheid Schooling in America*, Jonathan Kozol writes how a high school in Chicago partnered with Hyatt Hotels to embed a "Culinary Arts" program into the high school curriculum.[22] Such programs can attract students who have little hope of attending college, but it does not mean it is the right program for the student. High school should be a time for student exploration into a variety of careers. School-to-work seems more appropriate at the community college level, and students should be permitted to choose according to what work is available and what they find most appealing.

## DROPOUTS

Sometimes public schools are called "dropout factories." Johns Hopkins University researchers coined this term for schools where "no more than 60% of the students who start as freshmen make it to their senior year."[23] Teachers are blamed for students who leave school early, but students drop out of school for a variety of reasons, some due to the current policies championed by the individuals who criticize the dropout rate! The term "pushed out" has been coined by those who believe students drop out because they are not provided the help they really need in charter schools.

The dropout rate is questioned, too. Sometimes schools have poor recording practices, or school administrators fail to correctly track students. Students may have enrolled in private or charter schools, or parents forget to inform school administrators when they move. Some students repeat a grade or grades and graduate later but are counted as dropouts in their original grade.

Lawrence Mishel and Joydeep Roy of the Economic Policy Institute point to an incorrect 50 percent graduation rate for minorities. They worry such mistakes encourage a mischaracterization of black students as lacking achievement or being nonparticipants in school (2007). Three out of four black youths obtain diplomas, and 13 percent go on to receive GEDs. The dropout problem only affects about 20 percent of high schools, and when students do drop out it is often due to poverty.

Schools that keep students motivated and interested are what is needed, but calling schools dropout factories will not help. Students are more likely to care about attending a school they feel proud of—not schools repeatedly vilified by outsiders who know little about them or their schools.

## THE MILITARY

> The relationship between Army recruiters and educators in a school district is a potential source of comfort and conflict for both parties. Before you can expect any type of assistance from school officials or be accepted by students you must first establish rapport and credibility. You must convince them that you have their students' best interests in mind. They need to know that your interest in their students goes beyond enlisting them and extends to a genuine concern for their future.
>
> —School Recruiting Program Handbook[24]

Military recruitment is part of career exploration in America's public high schools, but little mention is made of closing the gap between rich and poor. In 2005, *New York Times* columnist Bob Herbert wrote, "Stop fighting unnecessary wars, or reinstate the draft."[25] Herbert goes on to note how young people are relentlessly recruited from rural and urban neighborhoods. Fewer students enlist from wealthy families.

No Child Left Behind provision Section 9528 gave the armed forces access to a student's personal information, requiring public schools to allow military recruiting. Public schools receive federal funds for carrying out this provision. Pressured with dwindling budgets, principals assist in meeting this quota in several ways.

The Armed Services Vocational Aptitude Battery Career Exploration Program, otherwise known as the ASVAB-CEP or ASVAB, is an admissions and placement test to determine student career interests, strengths, and qualification for the military. The ASVAB is not new. It has been around since 1968. But new privacy concerns have surfaced about the way the test is administered and how the information is used.

Absent bubbling in Option 8, a student's information becomes the property of the Department of Defense (DoD). By taking the test, students provide address, phone number, age, grade, ethnicity and racial data, email addresses, birth dates, grade point averages, test scores, and plans they might have for after graduation. Bubbling in Option 8 on the test answer sheet blocks military access. Students and parents are not always aware of this choice. And parents and students should check to make sure Option 8 is still used as a block in their schools.

In 1974, the Family Educational Rights and Privacy Act stood in the way of the DoD obtaining highly personal information from schools, but that is no longer the case. The only way students will not share their data is if they bubble Option 8. If not, their information will go to recruiters and be stored in a DoD database.

In 2005, Baltimore parent John Schneider was stunned to find that few other parents knew about the military opt-out provision of the ASVAB. Schneider and friends learned many high schools did not have an opt-out test provision. Students believed they had to take the test. Schneider's group pushed for better uniform procedures so as to ensure students could correctly opt out.

Since then, Maryland has become the only state to enact a law prohibiting the automatic release, through the ASVAB, of a student's personal information to military recruiters (National Coalition to Protect Student Privacy). Californians also tried to pass such a bill in that state, but then governor Arnold Schwarzenegger vetoed the bill. In Maryland, students and families can share personal information from the test with the military only if the student chooses to enlist. But in other states, how the ASVAB is administered is anyone's guess.

Seventeen- and eighteen-year-olds are still young, so parents must find how the ASVAB is handled in their student's high school. In some places, opt-out forms are mixed in with dozens of papers for the new school year, so it is easy to either lose the paper or not understand its significance. It is also possible that patriotic principals and teachers will encourage students to take the test without mentioning Option 8.

Some students feel ashamed if they *do not* take the test. Seventeen-year-olds may not sign up for military service without parent permission. But if students are convinced they want to join, it can be tough for parents to say no.

Because the test relies heavily on career aspirations, students might be led to believe that by joining the military they will eventually be able to get to college. That dream might otherwise not be a reality due to a family's poor financial resources. Students also take many tests in school. If the ASVAB is the only test where they receive positive feedback, it might be hard not to feel positive about enlisting in the armed services.

In addition to ASVAB testing, students might be persuaded to join the military when military recruiters visit the school. As noted in *The State*, in South Carolina:

> Earning money for college while traveling around the world, driving Humvees and jumping out of airplanes can be attractive to a high school student. However, recruiters, posters and advertisements accentuate the positive and exaggerate the potential benefits. When recruiters (with glossy posters and exciting slogans) say you can get up to $70,000 for college, they seldom stress such a large amount of money is only available for GIs who take military jobs that are difficult to fill. Nor do they stress that in order to qualify for any aid at all, you must pay a $1,200 nonrefundable fee to the military.[26]

Recruiters can become entrenched in the school. The following list, found in the handbook, of what recruiters should do to facilitate school visits was circulated on the Internet:

- Be so helpful and so much a part of the school scene that you are in constant demand.
- Cultivate coaches, librarians, administrative staff, and teachers.
- Know your student influencers. Students such as class officers, newspaper and yearbook editors, and athletes can help build interest in the army among the student body.
- Distribute desk calendars to your assigned schools.
- Attend athletic events at the high school. Make sure you wear your uniform.
- Get involved with the parent-teacher association.
- Coordinate with school officials to eat lunch in the school cafeteria several times each month.
- Deliver doughnuts and coffee for the faculty once a month.
- Coordinate with the homecoming committee to get involved with the parade.
- Get involved with the local Boy Scouts. Many scouts are high school students and potential enlistees or student influencers.
- Order personal presentation items (pens, bags, mousepads, mugs) as needed monthly for special events.
- Attend as many school holiday functions or assemblies as possible.

- Offer to be a timekeeper at football games.
- Martin Luther King Jr.'s birthday is in January. Wear your dress blues and participate in school events commemorating this holiday. February . . . Black History Month. Participate in events as available.
- Contact the high school athletic director and arrange for an exhibition basketball game between the faculty and army recruiters.[27]

Leave My Child Alone is a website providing information about how to opt out of the high school ASVAB and the national JAMRS (Joint Advertising Marketing and Research Services)—the military recruitment database. They provide forms that can be freely downloaded, filled out, and turned to the high school.

Public schools must better address a variety of career and vocational paths for all students, especially those who have difficulties in school. High schools should forecast realistic career opportunities. The decision to join the military ought to be based on serious consideration, personal interest preferably with family support, and a realistic understanding of what is involved.

## CONCLUSION: CAREERS

Instead of the narrow one-size-fits-all approach to schooling, more consideration should be given to helping students realistically address today's job market. Students who do not wish to pursue a four-year college degree should learn about other options. School districts should be up to date on career forecasting.

But great care should be taken to determine what opportunities exist for the student. High school teachers and career counselors must be available to work closely with students to help them learn about the kinds of careers and jobs that exist. Students would benefit with classes that help them to understand more about their academic strengths and weaknesses.

Another positive development is that college leaders are beginning to look differently at admission requirements for students. Instead of focusing on SAT and ACT scores and a laundry list of service activities, they are looking more closely at individual students and their strengths and passions. Here is the revised list of what they deem important in college admissions:

1. Contributions to one's family
2. Assessing students' daily awareness of and contributions to others

3. Prioritizing quality—not quantity—of activities
4. Awareness of overloading on AP/IB courses
5. Discouraging "overcoaching"
6. Options for reducing test pressure
7. Expanding students' thinking about "good" colleges[28]

Could we see the breakup of high-stakes testing in high schools in the near future? What significance will this have on high-stakes testing in elementary and middle school?

While the job outlook at the time of this writing is weak, and the serious loan and debt crisis facing college students is bleak, public schools can still go a long way toward helping young people find the careers for which they might be suited. Students need assistance understanding the kinds of scholarships that are available and how to navigate the university application process.

Narrowing the scope of what is offered in school with high-stakes standardization—teaching and overtesting students—ignores the potential in America's students.

Public high schools should also expand curriculum offerings. Programs to address individual interests and future opportunities should be a part of every student's school regimen—especially in high school. Students need to understand the choices that are available, but it is the student, after careful guidance, who should ultimately decide his or her best career path.

## NOTES

1. Gerald Bracey, "Believing the Worst About Schools: A Lack of Logic from *Sputnik* to *Tough Choices*," Huff Post: Politics, December 17, 2006, http://www.huffingtonpost.com/gerald-bracey/believing-the-worst-about_b_36562.html.

2. Alan S. Blinder, "Free Trade's Great, but Offshoring Rattles Me," *Washington Post*, May 6, 2007.

3. Richard Rothstein, "A Distraction from Schools' Real Needs," *School Administrator* 64, no. 9 (2007): 6.

4. Marc. Tucker, "Making Tough Choices," *Phi Delta Kappan* 88, no. 10 (2007): 728–32.

5. Marc S. Tucker, National Center on Education and the Economy, http://www.ncee.org/about-ncee/our-people/leadership/marc-s-tucker/.

6. "The Marc Tucker 'Dear Hillary' Letter," Eagle Forum, http://www.eagleforum.org/educate/marc_tucker/.

7. Phyllis Shalafly, "Marc Tucker Re-Emerges to Present a Warmed-Over Plan," Townhall, January 23, 2007, http://townhall.com/columnists/phyllisschlafly/2007/01/23/marc_tucker_re-emerges_to_present_a_warmed-over_plan/page/full.

8. Phyllis Schlafly, "Why the Public Schools Are Being Federalized," *Eagle Forum* 33, no. 9 (April 2000), http://www.eagleforum.org/psr/2000/apr00/psrapr2000.html.

9. Lawrence Mishel and Richard Rothstein, "Improper Diagnosis, Reckless Treatment," *Phi Delta Kappan* 89, no. 1 (2007): 32.

10. Jeffrey Selingo, "Work-Force Panel Calls for Overhaul of U.S. Education," *Chronicle of Higher Education* 53, no. 18 (2007): 1.

11. Vicki Phillips and Carina Wong, "Tying Together the Common Core of Standards, Instruction, and Assessments," *Phi Delta Kappan* 91, no. 5 (2010): 37–42.

12. Marc Tucker, "Annual Accountability Testing: Time for the Civil Rights Community to Reconsider," *Education Week*, May 28, 2015, http://blogs.edweek.org/edweek/top_performers/2015/05/annual_accountability_testing_time_for_the_civil_rights_community_to_reconsider.html?r=1585753796.

13. Lawrence Mishel, Josh Bivens, Elise Gould, and Heidi Shierholz, *The State of Working America*, Economic Policy Institute (Ithaca, NY: Cornell University Press, 2012), 366.

14. Barbara Ehrenreich, "The Apocalypse Is Yours Now," Haverford College Commencement Speech, Sunday, May 20, Barbara's Blog, May 21, 2007.

15. Paul E. Barton, "How Many College Graduates Does the U.S. Labor Force Really Need?" *Change*, www.changemag.org/Archives/Back%20Issues/January-February%202008/abstract-how-many-graduates.html.

16. Presidential Remarks at Business Roundtable, February 24, 2010, http://www.c-spanvideo.org/videoLibrary/transcript/transcript.php?programid=220104.

17. CNN Transcripts, CNN Newsroom, "Sally Ride's New Mission," September 16, 2010, http://archives.cnn.com/TRANSCRIPTS/1009/16/cnr.06.html.

18. Ibid.

19. Improving the Laboratory Experience for America's High School Students, Subcommittee on Research and Science Education Committee on Science and Technology, House of Representatives, March 8, 2007, http://commdocs.house.gov/committees/science/hsy33612.000/hsy33612_0f.htm.

20. Al Baker, "Obama, at Brooklyn School, Pushes Education Agenda," *New York Times*, October 25, 2013.

21. Ibid.

22. Jonathan Kozol, *The Shame of the Nation: The Restoration of Apartheid Schooling in America* (New York: Crown, 2005), 102–3.

23. Nancy Zuckerbrod, "1 in 10 Schools Are 'Dropout Factories,'" *USA Today*, November 9, 2007.

24. School Recruiting Program Handbook, USAREC Pamphlet 350-13, Chapter 2, School Relations, http://www.grassrootspeace.org/army_recruiter_hdbk.pdf.

25. Bob Herbert, "Truth in Recruiting," *New York Times*, August 22, 2005.

26. Michael Berg, "Military Recruiters Have Unrivaled Access to Schools," *The State* (South Carolina), February 23, 2005.

27. Sheldon Rampton, "War Is Fun as Hell," The Center for Media and Democracy's PR Watch, July 27, 2005, http://www.prwatch.org/node/3865.

28. Richard Weissbourd, Lloyd Thacker, Trisha Ross Anderson, Alison Cashin, Luba Falk Feigenberg, and Jennifer Kahn, "Turning the Tide: Inspiring Concern for Others and the Common Good through College Admissions," Harvard Graduate School of Education. 2014, http://mcc.gse.harvard.edu/collegeadmissions.

## *Chapter Four*

# Religion's Threat to Public Schools

> I contemplate with sovereign reverence that act of the whole American people which [built] . . . a wall of separation between church and state.
>
> —Thomas Jefferson

## HORACE MANN

Because America is a democracy and public schools instruct students with diverse backgrounds and religious beliefs, it is not possible nor should we wish to accommodate religion in one public school setting. This is one of the reasons why separation of church and state is important. But some religious leaders and followers dislike the idea of tax dollars going to schools that do not follow their particular church dogma.

Controversy concerning religion in public schools increased after the US Supreme Court's decision in 1963 to ban public school prayer, and also with the *Roe v. Wade* abortion decision in 1973 (Doyle, 2003). Resurgence in religious fundamentalism followed as Evangelicals vied to get religion in public schools while supporters of separation of church and state aimed to not entangle religion with learning. Consequently, public schools have become a religious battleground, and religion stands to undue the democratic principles public schools once embraced.

A 2001 Supreme Court decision concerning *The Good News Club v. Milford Central School* opened the door to serious evangelism in public schools (Tabachnick, 2012). Now, the Child Evangelism Fellowship (CEF) has set up Good News Clubs in schools across the country, teaching students through pamphlets, treats, and proselytizing that they risk going to hell if they do not join the club (Stewart, 2009).

Public schools and religion have been a difficult mix from the start. Horace Mann, considered the father of public education, envisioned a country where poor and elite could be educated together in an attempt for economic equalization. While growing up, Mann attended a Calvinist Congregational Church where the popular pastor preached hell and damnation (Ritchie, 1999–2013). When Horace's older brother Stephen died in a drowning accident, the pastor's fiery funeral service about hell for the unconverted dead proved too much for Mann. He left the church and eventually became a Unitarian. Some Baptists still see that conversion as anti-Christian.

Mann stressed character virtues such as piety and love of country, but knowing many parents wanted religion in school, he quipped, "Are not these virtues and graces part and parcel of Christianity?"[1] Some believe today's character programs are born from Mann's reasoning. But others accuse Mann of ignoring religion, and he is often blamed for making schools humanistic and secular. This may contribute to the dislike of public schools by Evangelicals today. Mann, believing schools would not survive without a Protestant regimen, included the Bible in schools, mostly to appease parents.

But the reliance early schools had on puritanical biblical teaching had disastrous consequences for Irish Catholics in Massachusetts. Catholic children attending public schools faced ridicule as they were forced to read the King James Bible and participate in other Protestant rituals. Student textbooks included anti-Catholic passages.

Outraged parents pulled their children from school, and parental opposition contributed to the Philadelphia Bible Riots and the burning of a Catholic church. School officials eventually removed the offensive reading material (Kaestle, 2001, 33–38). A new Board of Education in New York City and an influential archbishop opened Catholic schools. But the early ostracism of Catholics from public schools remains an example of what can happen when one religious group dominates.

This failure on the part of Mann's common school plan allowed for religious discord in the early years of public schooling. Yet the basic premise of common schools to educate children, no matter their socioeconomic background, is a powerful concept. For this, much credit is attributed to Horace Mann.

## CHURCHES

> I hope I live to see the day when, as in the early days of our country, we won't have any public schools. The churches will have taken them over again and Christians will be running them. What a happy day that will be.
>
> —Reverend Jerry Falwell[2]

Some Southern Baptists want to change public schools to accommodate fundamentalist beliefs. In 2005, public schools were high on the agenda of the Southern Baptist Convention (SBC). MSNBC reported the group was in the "doldrums" (i.e., baptisms were down and the church had problems enrolling new members), and Rev. Bobby Welch of the First Baptist Church said, "The convention will be united on the fact that our school system is in terrible disrepair and in a critical and urgent need for help." He added, "do not believe that most Southern Baptists believe that just a wholesale, universal call for a withdrawing of students from public schools is the best answer."[3]

Earlier it had been suggested that parents remove children from public schools. But expensive private schools and a reliance on homeschooling proved difficult. The new plan encouraged members to infiltrate school districts with what President Reverend Welch called "change agents in a world and a society that many times is totally ungodly."[4] The Religious Right also works together with free market supporters in a strange alliance to denounce public schools (Martin, 2014, 46). Both seek the replacement of public schools with charter schools and vouchers.

R. Albert Mohler Jr., ninth president of the Southern Baptist Theological Seminary in Louisville, Kentucky and board member for James Dobson's Focus on the Family, first preached in favor of an exodus, and Harvard and Stanford educated Bruce Shortt prodded: "What Baptists need to do now is create a new public education system, a system that is public in the sense that it is open to everyone and that takes into account the needs of orphans, single parents, and the disadvantaged. With our existing buildings, our talented people, and the educational technology available today, it is now possible to create rapidly and affordable, effective Christian education alternative to the government schools."[5]

The Christian Educators Association International (CEAI) is a part of the religious plan to create Christian schools. Claiming to be the only professional association for Christians who work in public school settings, they describe as their mission: "To Encourage, Equip and Empower Educators according to Biblical Principles."[6] Supported by membership dues, tax-deductible donations, and grants, CEAI is open to teachers, administrators, para-professionals, and anyone employed by the school district. The group promises to "Preserve our Judeo-Christian heritage and values through education." They stress belief in one God, the Bible, and the need for a spiritual conversion.

Training religious educators to enter public schools with a focus on conversion is more common than many might think. In 2009, Christian *World* magazine reported that 50 percent of Teach for America's (TFA) incoming corps members actively participated in a church or other faith community (Harris, 2009). One TFA group cited faith as a motivating factor for joining TFA. TFA states they respect the separation of church and state, but they recruit from the Christian organization Young Life. Young Life partners with adults who build faith relationships with adolescents. In some charter schools, TFA appears like missionaries serving the poor.

*World* also tells about some of the Christian universities that spread faith-based messages intended to infiltrate public schools:

- Trinity International University in Lincolnshire, Illinois, sends students to local public high schools to do undergraduate student teaching. Public school students may visit students at TIU, and the professors are planning guest lectures at the high schools.
- Union University in Memphis, Tennessee, "partners with a local faith-based organization and the secular Urban Teacher Residency United Network to create the Memphis Teacher Residency Program pairing applicants with inner-city classroom mentors. The Memphis Teacher Residency program is the only Christian one of its kind, integrating faith with the classes and holding devotionals each week."
- Eastern University is "a Christian university in St. Davids, Pennsylvania," near Philadelphia. It took "a grant from a subsidiary of the Bill and Melinda Gates Foundation to start the Eastern University Academy Charter School."
- George Fox University is a Quaker university in Newberg, Oregon, which "works with public-school districts to identify future teacher leaders and train them to get their administrators licenses."[7]

Though Reverend Jerry Falwell, a serious critic of public schools, did not live to see them converted into Christian schools, significant strides have been taken in that direction. The Southern Baptist mission influences curriculum and leadership. Evangelicals seek election to the legislature, school board, or attempt to acquire school administration appointments. Through high-level positions and obtaining jurisdiction over curriculum, the Religious Right alters school management and influences how and what students are taught.

Some of serious controversies surrounding public schools and religion involve:

- School prayer and Bible study
- Character education
- Creationism or intelligent design versus evolution
- Sex education

Southern Baptists are not the only religious organization jockeying to influence public schools. Muslims want their own schools. Catholics have parochial schools, and, like most religions, they support school vouchers to get public funding. Those who favor working from within public schools in order to convert them, and those who stress removing students, go far in instilling in the public an overall hostile outlook toward public education.

Past religious battles should make it understandable as to why courts tread carefully when it comes to religion and schooling, but ongoing attempts by the Religious Right continue to dismantle public schools and/or reshape them to reflect religious ideology. Their influence can be easily spotted in the day-to-day business of converting public schools to charter schools—many of which are now run by religious organizations.

## CHARTER SCHOOLS

> It is the gnomes which, in a spiritual way, make good in the world what the lower orders of the animals up to the amphibians lack. This applies also to the fishes, which have only indications of the skeleton. These lower animal orders only become complete, as it were, through the fact that gnomes exist.
>
> —Rudolf Steiner, founder of Waldorf Schools[8]

> Whenever we remove a brick from the wall that was designed to separate religion and government, we increase the risk of religious strife and weaken the foundation of our democracy.
>
> —Supreme Court justice John Paul Stephens, *Zelman v. Simmons-Harris*

Joe Nathan, prominent in the development of charter schools, wrote about charter schools, vouchers, and religion in a 2005 article, "Charter's 'Yes!' Vouchers 'No!'":

> Faith-based schools are established to, among other things, promote a religion. One of the ways they do that is to show how their religion, whether it is Lutheran, Jewish, Catholic, Muslim, Hindu, or whatever, is superior to any and all others . . . as I see it, while a school might also try to teach tolerance, the bottom line for most religious schools is the promotion of one religion over all others. America already is an enormously diverse country and is becoming more so all the time. By and large we have avoided the centuries-long religious battles that we see in places like Ireland, the Middle East, and the Balkans. No one knows for certain how much religious schools have contributed to those conflicts, but materials from religious schools in those areas have been examined, and some are quite inflammatory.[9]

Nathan's points about religion and schooling are important, but forgotten. Religious charter schools are increasing, and the rules surrounding how they are governed are murky. Ministers run many charter schools. Conditions NCLB described pertaining to charter schools and religion included:

- Faith-based and religious organizations are allowed to be involved with charter schools.
- Charter schools may teach values reflecting the religious viewpoint of the school but may not provide religious instruction. They may teach religion from a secular viewpoint.
- All activities are supposed to be nonreligious.
- Charter schools can be housed in church facilities.
- Public funds are not to be used for religious activities.
- Business and community organizations can partner with religious organizations involving charter schools.
- Charter schools may carry out outreach and recruitment activities to reach the parent community. (2004)

How many NCLB rules concerning religion were broken? Charter schools sometimes involve problematic religious practices with tax dollars taken from public schools. The Texas Prepared Table Charter School received $20 million in public funds starting in 1998. Much of that money went to the church and salaries to the pastor and his wife, not to the charter school or students (Leaming, 2003). Church officials also tampered with attendance records to obtain more funding. Once discovered, Texas charter school law did not require the church to pay back the money.

Unusual circumstances surround Waldorf schools. Parents who consider themselves progressive find in these schools some of what they used to love and now miss in overstandardized public schools. Waldorf waits until a child is older to teach reading, and they have a free-spirited art-based curriculum. Currently Waldorf has about one thousand schools around the world, including 159 schools in America. Forty-four Waldorf schools in the United States are charter schools (Costello-Dougherty, 2009). The school's philosophy follows a religion called Anthroposophy created by Austrian Rudolf Steiner.

Steiner believed in a spiritual world reachable through inner consciousness if humans would resist their focus on materialism. He warned "against a devilish spirit named Ahriman, who threatened the world; discussed the activities of the Buddha on Mars; advocated reading to the dead; accepted reincarnation and karma (the idea that actions in past lives affect present ones); and proclaimed acquaintance with the Akashic records of everything that has happened in the universe" (1861–1925).

The Waldorf program pulled the most attractive ideas of their founder to use in the schools. Waldorf trains teachers and awards them their own Waldorf degrees. Along with tax dollars for many US Waldorf charter schools, donations are also requested.

People for Legal and Nonsectarian Schools (PLANS), a website run by past Waldorf parents, provided information about the religious side of Waldorf schools. President Debra Snell says of Waldorf:

> I began to ask questions. What is Anthroposophy? Why don't teachers allow students in the preschool through the early elementary grades to use black crayons in their drawings? Why do students use the wet-on-wet watercolor painting technique exclusively for so many years? Why is mythology taught as history? Where is the American flag, and why don't Waldorf schools teach civics lessons in America? In a school system that promotes itself as "education toward freedom," why do students copy everything from the blackboard? Why do Waldorf teachers talk in high voices and singsong directions to their classes? Why must the kindergarten room walls be painted "peach blossom"? Why is learning to read before the age of 8 or 9 considered unhealthy? Why do so many Waldorf classes have problems with bullying, and what is the school's policy for dealing with this? Why are teachers always lighting candles?
>
> What answers I received were not forthright, and the teachers made it clear that my questions were not welcome. They told me, "If you understood

> Anthroposophy, you wouldn't be asking that question." Yet before we enrolled, I was told that the school was non-sectarian and that Anthroposophy was not "in the classroom!" I was eventually invited to leave.[10]

What do students learn in so many charter schools that eludes oversight? In 2000, a publicly financed charter school called National Heritage Academy in Rochester intended to teach creationism as a competing theory with evolution (Wyatt, 2000). Teaching creationism is controversial and generates concern at public school board meetings across the country and in the courts. But without public school boards, there is no debate.

The charter school chain, owned and operated under various names by National Heritage Academies (NHA), has, at this time, seventy-six for-profit schools in Colorado, Georgia, Indiana, Michigan, New York, North Carolina, Louisiana, Ohio, and Wisconsin. NHA is only one example of the many charter schools that include religious beliefs in the curriculum, yet are funded by tax dollars.

Gulen charter schools are one of the largest chain for-profit schools and have raised controversy. The *New York Times* reported that the schools' leaders follow Fethullah Gulen, a Turkish preacher building a "worldwide religious, social and nationalistic movement in his name," and in America, the schools hire many teachers and administrators from Turkey.[11] They also spend millions of dollars building new school facilities.

The lines involving separation of church and state concerning public schools has been redrawn with charter schools, opening a whole new dimension of misinformation and distrust. The progress made in the courts concerning separation of church and state is at risk. Little oversight of the spending practices involving religious charter schools exists, and many Americans might not understand how their tax dollars are being spent. Most troublesome is that segregated religious schools, no matter the religion, do little to bring children together.

## VOUCHERS

> When the government puts its imprimatur on a particular religion it conveys a message of exclusion to all those who do not adhere to the favored beliefs. A government cannot be premised on the belief that all persons are created equal when it asserts that God prefers some.
>
> —Supreme Court justice Harry A. Blackmun, *Agostini v. Felton*

> In the end, parents want the "choice" of a strong neighborhood school. They don't want to have to research the best elementary schools with nurses. They don't want to be forced to shop around for the best electives in middle schools or attend colossal school fairs to pick the best high school. Parents don't have the time nor do they want to become experts in determining which curriculum standards offered at which schools are best. Parents don't want to become private investigators tracking down who really owns their school or hunting down teaching credentials or financial liquidity of schools. They want their kids to go to a strong, high quality public school nearby. Period. That's the ultimate "choice" all parents really want. Each time you de-fund public education with legislation like this, you strip that choice away from parents. You weaken existing public schools vs. strengthening them.
>
> —Rita M. Solnet, president of Parents Across Florida[12]

Using vouchers is another way to dismantle public schools. Vouchers divert tax dollars to religious schools through payments to parents allowing them to place their children in private or charter schools. They were introduced in the 1950s by American economist Milton Friedman.

Voucher programs have been started in Milwaukee (1990), Cleveland (1995), Florida (1999), the District of Columbia (2004), and Louisiana (2012). In 2015, the Nevada Legislature passed the most extensive voucher program in the country. It involves Education Savings Accounts, which amount to $5,100 per child, which can be used for homeschooling or religious schools.

Vouchers deplete public schools of vital funding, cream good students from public schools, and provide financial incentives to those who are often already able to afford private school. Vouchers are worrisome when parents use them to enroll children in religious schools not open to other students. Like charter schools, many of these schools have little oversight, and it is difficult to know what a child will be taught and the kind of experience and preparation of the school staff.

In the 2013 *Phi Delta Kappan* "Gallup Poll of the Public's Attitudes toward the Public Schools," 70 percent of parents indicated they did not want vouchers (Bushaw and Lopez). So why are so many state legislators working hard to obtain them? Some parents who support vouchers argue that they pay taxes and deserve a portion of those dollars for their child's schooling. But funding public schools has always been about educating all children so the country will have an educated populace. Public schooling is a truly democratic institution, but these schools are jeopardized by charter schools and vouchers.

An often divided Supreme Court, however, has made the constitutionality of vouchers more favorable with rulings that include *Muller v. Allen* (1983), which allowed Minnesota parents to claim a tax deduction for private school attendance; and the controversial Supreme Court decision *Zelman v. Simmons-Harris* (2002), making vouchers available to disadvantaged parents in Cleveland ("Church, Choice, and Charters: A New Wrinkle for Public Education?" 2009).

Milwaukee's voucher program (where vouchers got their start) began in 1990 for poor students. Vouchers have not been successful there. Traditional public schools perform better, despite harmful budget cuts. In general, little evidence shows that voucher students do better in private schools than public schools. Education has not improved with the use of vouchers.

Nevertheless, the voucher program was expanded in 2011 with the help of Wisconsin's governor Scott Walker. Not only do students there attend private religious schools, but about 67 percent already attended the schools before they received the vouchers (Richards and Simonaitis, 2013). Milwaukee's voucher program is also no longer considered a program to assist disadvantaged students, instead becoming a state entitlement program.

Ohio's school system is one example of public/private and religious school conversion. Some 96 percent of students there use vouchers to attend private religious schools. Students in Academic Watch or Academic Emergency public schools are provided a scholarship that funds full or partial tuition to religious private schools, yet these schools are largely unaccountable to parents and students. Ohio also uses vouchers to send autistic children and students with disabilities to private schools. The kind of services these schools provide is not well known.

The Autistic Scholarship Program is problematic because it excludes students with severe disabilities and students not of the same religion affiliated to the school (Lier, 2008). In some cases, parents pay more than the provided voucher amount, and students relinquish their right to special education protections under the law. Students with disabilities are also instructed separately from those without disabilities, unlike inclusion favored in public schools. Also, in 2013, Ohio's voucher program showed no sign of improving services for disadvantaged students or students with autism, yet the state's EdChoice voucher program expanded to include disadvantaged students attending high-performing public schools (Bloom, 2013).

Washington, DC's voucher program passed in 2004 by only one vote in the House of Representatives and was the first federally funded school voucher program. Around 82 percent of voucher students there attend religious schools. Like other voucher schools, private religious schools accepting government voucher money, unlike public schools, are not held accountable for student learning. Americans United for Separation of Church and State claim vouchers divert "desperately needed resources away from the public school system to fund the education of the few voucher students," and the DC voucher program has similarly not improved student performance. It serves "mainly to subsidize religious education with tax funds."[13]

Florida's Department of Education lists four voucher scholarship programs:

- The Florida Tax Credit Scholarship Program (2001) awards scholarships to children from low-income families that come from state tax credits for contributions to nonprofit scholarship-finding organizations (SFOs).
- The McKay Scholarship Fund for Students with Disabilities permits parents with students who have special needs to receive funds to transfer students to a charter or private school or to another public school. Over thirty thousand students participated in 2014 to 2015 school year.
- The Opportunity Scholarship Program offers students who attend public schools deemed to be failing the option to attend a higher-performing school or private school.
- The Personal Learning Scholarships Accounts (PLSA) program is administered by state-approved nonprofit Scholarship Funding Organizations to provide the parents the option to purchase certain services or products.

In 1999, Florida instituted the McKay Scholarship Program by insisting public schools could not help all students with disabilities and vouchers to private schools were needed. But most private schools lack the necessary teachers and services to address disabilities. Some of the programs have been fraught with corruption. Many parents used the vouchers to place their children in religious, unaccredited schools with no specialized education programs. Permission to obtain vouchers was derived by Governor Jeb Bush's school grading plan based on scores from the Florida Comprehensive Assessment Test.

In 2006, the Florida Supreme Court struck down the Governor's Opportunity Scholarship Program, which would have provided vouchers to private schools for failing public school students. But to get around this decision, Bush worked with neoconservative allies, also voucher proponents. They went through the Taxation and Budget Reform Commission to approve vouchers. Patricia Levesque, a neoconservative graduate of the religious fundamentalist Bob Jones University, currently serves as executive director of Bush's provoucher Foundation for Florida's Future as well as his Foundation for Excellence in Education. Both groups are committed to privatizing public schools.

In 2011, Gus Garcia-Roberts of the *Miami New Times News* won an award for exposing the corruption surrounding vouchers in Florida, including the McKay Scholarship Program. Out of 1,013 schools receiving vouchers in 2011, 65 percent were religious schools. The programs were riddled with problems.

South Florida Preparatory Christian Academy had no curriculum and was located over a liquor store near a massage parlor. The Florida Department of Education never visited the school, which offered no curriculum. It was so unsafe it eventually had to be condemned. The owner of the school, once a basketball coach, received $2 million for students in the schools with disabilities and an additional $236,000 for low-income students through a state tax-credit scholarship. This is just one of many stories Garcia-Roberts exposed.

Voucher schools are not like public schools, and the following differences show how they run by different rules and lack transparency:

1. Students do not have to take standardized tests.
2. Teachers do not have to have education degrees or state credentials.
3. There is no fiscal accountability.
4. The diversion of funds destroys traditional public school programs.
5. Funding still flows to religious schools even though voters voted against it.
6. Not all children are accepted. (Solnet, 2014)

Another school voucher program in Louisiana pulls in about half that state's poor and middle-class students. This includes Bible-based schools that teach creationism. These schools are antiscience, antihistory, and have little oversight. A college student named Zack Kopplin pushed back on vouchers with a Change.org petition. He collected seventy thousand signatures—an indication that not everyone in Louisiana is in favor of vouchers.

But religious schools there are still much in play. These schools base their curriculum on the Beka Book from Bob Jones University Press. It teaches students that dragons are real, man coexisted with dinosaurs, and the Trail of

Tears was devised by God to convert Native Americans to Christianity (Pan, 2012).

Despite corruption surrounding private religious school vouchers in Florida, many GOP state legislators now support Step Up for Students, education credit vouchers to send children to private or parochial schools:

> The current cap on tax credits is set at $286 million. It funds about 60,000 scholarships annually. The cap is already scheduled to grow to $874 million over the next five years. But lawmakers are considering a bill (SB 1620, HB 7099) that would enable the program to grow more quickly than it otherwise would.[14]

Floridians might be deceived into thinking vouchers are off the table when they are only switched to another program. In 2014, the bill to expand vouchers in the legislature appeared to fail but was converted into the Florida Tax Credit Scholarship. Such programs are gaining popularity as a way for individuals and corporations to use scholarship programs to get students into private schools, thereby forwarding choice. Taxpayers and corporations opt into the program in order to contribute to the school of their choice and then get tax breaks on their donations (Ash, 2014). In Pennsylvania, similar programs are called REACH and Educational Improvement Tax Credit.

Vouchers have not improved student scores and have failed at a high cost to taxpayers and students (Ravitch, 2013, 210). Yet vouchers continue to be supported by religious leaders and business groups who see it as a legitimate practice to divert tax dollars to the ultimate religious privatization of America's public schools. Many school voucher bills are currently and most likely will continue to be hotly debated in states such as Tennessee, Hawaii, Alaska, Indiana, and, of course, Florida.

## CHARACTER EDUCATION

> Character education's history in the United States goes back to the beginning of public schools. The emphasis and profile has waxed and waned, frequently with political trends. The current standards-based environment poses particular threats and challenges to character education.
>
> —Robert W. Howard, Marvin W. Berkowitz, and Esther F. Schaeffer[15]

Many see building character in school as an important goal, and teaching morals or virtues and patriotism in school is nothing new. An umbrella of character programs can be found in schools today, including: antibullying, antidrug, virtue-of-the-month studies, and a push for students to commit to service activities. Educators, philosophers, theologians, and psychologists have always pondered how to instill moral behavior in young people. But it always comes back to this question, who should decide what makes good character?

Character education is political. For some, obedience is important. For others, challenging authority is good character. When Mia Kang of MacArthur High School in San Antonio, Texas, used her practice test bubble answer sheet form to write an essay challenging standardized testing, some called it disobedient—others courageous (LaCoste-Caputo, 2005).

Character education changes with the times. In the 1950s, moral education emphasized obedience. By the 1960s and 1970s, character education moved toward making choices. But that would not last.

In 1992, Howard Kirschenbaum, educational psychologist and professor emeritus of the department of Counseling and Human Development at the University of Rochester, wrote about how a book he coauthored called *Values Clarification: A Handbook of Practical Strategies for Teachers and Students*, which introduced students to thought-provoking situations, suddenly lost popularity.

Obedience advocates worried about permissiveness, so the 1980s saw the pendulum swing back to an emphasis on student compliance. Kirschenbaum said, "The relatively permissive, hopeful, idealistic Sixties and Seventies gave way to the more politically conservative, economically fearful, and socially disintegrating Eighties."[16]

In recent years, school districts have looked to outside partnerships and nonprofit groups to provide the character goals that they conclude children should learn in school. Presidents from both political parties have endorsed these groups and their style of character education, yet such organizations and individuals could have their own political slant toward character education.

William Bennett, education czar under President Reagan, who promoted character education by rewriting fables in *The Book of Virtues: A Treasury of Great Moral Stories*, has also been one of the harshest critics of public schools. He shared his support of character education, however, with President Bill Clinton, who, in his 1996 State of the Union address, said, "I challenge all our schools to teach character education, to teach good values, and good citizenship."[17] Clinton's Goals 2000 included an emphasis on character education.

Some see character programs as having the premise that parents fail to teach values. Children are seen as immoral, so schools must offer prescribed programs to teach children how to behave. Character education in this case is about discipline.

Rod Paige, who was the first education secretary under President George W. Bush, said in 2003:

> Overall, we are failing to foster good character. In some schools, gangster rap and criminal deeds are tolerated, even allowed to replace education itself. We have to teach tolerance. But we do not have to tolerate the absence of positive values. For all these reasons, there is a dire need for the Character Education Partnership. We must teach our children more than reading and math; we must also teach them the values upon which this nation was built.[18]

The Character Education Partnership (CEP, or character.org) to which Paige refers promotes eleven principles believed necessary for good character. The CEP has ties to corporate sponsors, psychologists, and the military. General Colin Powell, former US Secretary of State, has been an active supporter of the CEP. A variety of current and past CEOs are on the board. Mr. Walter Isaacson, president and chief executive officer of the Aspen Institute, which often hosts speakers and books who promote school privatization, is also on the board.

In 1992, the Josephson Institute participated at the Aspen Summit Conference. Character Counts! refers to the Josephson Institute's character programs. It has been one of the more popular character programs found in public schools across the country. Michael Josephson is a former law professor, attorney, and president of the Character Counts! Coalition.

In 2000, Josephson wrote a white paper to President George W. Bush's Transition Team on Education concerning character education. He made several requests, including increased character education funding, to at least $24 million per year, and to increase faith-based involvement in after-school programs (Josephson, 2000). It is unclear how much money Character Counts! receives. Schools usually obtain grants, and the program now advertises how it will work with Common Core.

In 2001, President George W. Bush proclaimed October 27, 2001, as National Character Counts! Week. Bush heralded America's founders at Valley Forge and those who fought at Normandy and the deserts of the Persian Gulf. He referred to the nation's character after "the terrible terrorist attacks of September 11 . . . " and grouping government, the military, war, religion, and politics, he called for public school character education.[19]

In 2008, the "Josephson Institute's Report Card on American Youth: There's a Hole in Our Moral Ozone and It's Getting Bigger" claimed twenty-nine thousand students revealed "entrenched habits of dishonesty in the workforce of the future."[20] According to the paper, stealing, lying, and cheating were rising at "alarming rates," and students did not notice.

But the questions were tricky (who has never lied?), and the article created a backlash since it involved students in both public and private schools. The survey also raised questions surrounding the Josephson Institute's attempt to market their character program. Do parents and school officials require convincing that students need character programs to fix bad behavior?

Still, President Barack Obama has been a fan of Character Counts! Week, which occurs every year late in October. He has called for officials, educators, parents, students, and all Americans to hold ceremonies and activities (Josephson, 2012). Likely, activities and programs involve Josephson's materials and curriculum. The Senate also embraced Josephson's Character Counts! Week.

Education writer Alfie Kohn believes positive programs to address character should focus on accommodating children and their changing needs, instead of implying children need to be repaired. He states:

> What goes by the name of character education nowadays is, for the most part, a collection of exhortations and extrinsic inducements designed to make children work harder and do what they're told. Even when other values are also promoted—caring or fairness, say—the preferred method of instruction is tantamount to indoctrination. The point is to drill students in specific behaviors rather than to engage them in deep, critical reflection about certain ways of being. This is the impression one gets from reading articles and books by

> contemporary proponents of character education as well as the curriculum materials sold by the leading national programs. The impression is only strengthened by visiting schools that have been singled out for their commitment to character education.[21]

Similar to this concept, Lawrence Kohlberg, an American psychologist who studied moral development, revised the work of Swiss psychologist Jean Piaget and focused more on the reasoning behind character (McLeod, 2011). Kohlberg emphasized that children progress through stages where they acquire and internalize moral thinking in order to ascend to the next stage of moral development, and that this continues through adulthood. The knowledge that children learn character through developmental stages provides a more complete picture of moral development.

It suggests that character development might be best handled and be more interesting to young people through exposure to literature, the arts, science, social studies, and history. Through the use of nonfabricated character lessons or goals, students would have to formulate their own conclusions about what they read and study. Teachers might assist students in finding meaning within the school environment.

In literature, for example, the novel *Les Miserables* raises questions whether it is wrong for Jean Valjean to steal bread to feed his starving family. *The Diary of Anne Frank* provides lessons about courage, faith, and tolerance. Shel Silverstein's *The Giving Tree* teaches young and old how it feels when you love without receiving love in return. Such books raise questions that, like real-life situations, might not have set-in-stone answers.

But character education in public schools, and all schools, will continue to be debated. Adults should approach the issue of character education carefully. The best character education for students is most likely what they observe in the adults working and living among them.

## CONCLUSION: SEPARATION OF CHURCH AND STATE

Despite the fact that America is religiously diverse, many tax-supported programs support student attendance at religious schools. This is often the case with unregulated charter schools and vouchers.

But parents and educators are pushing back. Citizens who care about public schools can be found in every community. When the State of Nevada began permitting vouchers of $5,100 per child, Ruby Duncan, eighty-three, along with four other activists and the American Civil Liberties Union of

Nevada, sued. Duncan, who also fought for welfare benefits for single mothers, has an elementary school in her name (Sullivan, 2015).

But a lack of tolerance can occur in traditional public schools as well. In 2014, the ACLU of Louisiana sued on behalf of a sixth-grade Buddhist student of Thai descent, ridiculed for his religious beliefs.

The student, chastised by teachers and administrators in his public school and pressured to accept their beliefs, filed the suit. "When we filed the lawsuit, many people were shocked by the allegations. In addition to denigrating the student's Buddhist faith by calling it 'stupid,' school officials suggested he should transfer to another school with 'more Asians.' They also taught creationism in science class, incorporated prayer into class and nearly every school event, hung a portrait of Jesus over the main entryway, and participated in a number of other activities that blatantly violated the separation of church and state."[22]

A federal district court ordered the school district to refrain from using religion to ridicule students with different religious beliefs. The staff was ordered to attend in-service training concerning religious diversity. The family continued to be harassed, but the attention surrounding this situation might have enlightened others to be more tolerant.

In public schools, learning about different religions in social studies could assist students and educators to build tolerance toward each other (Rosenblith and Bailey, 2007). Such religious study programs help students understand traditions and beliefs found in other cultures. This assists students to build respect for peers who believe differently, and helps them understand the diverse world in which they live. It makes sense if public schools are to remain democratic institutions in a country that values religious freedom.

## NOTES

1. Horace Mann, "Twelfth Annual Report (1848) Moral Education, Political Education, and the Relation of Church, State, and Public School in a Free Society," in *The Republic and the School: Horace Mann on the Education of Free Men*, ed. Lawrence A. Cremin (New York: Columbia University, 1957), 106.

2. Jerry Falwell, *America Can Be Saved!* (Murfreesboro, TN: Sword of the Lord Publishers, 1979), 52–53.

3. Alex Johnson, "Southern Baptists in 'Doldrums,' Leader Says," MSNBC, June 17, 2005, http://www.msnbc.msn.com/id/8234284/.

4. Ibid.

5. Drew Zahn, "Southern Baptists: Finally Fed Up with Public School?" WorldNetDailey, March 31, 2009, http://www.wnd.com/index.php?pageId=99793.

6. Christian Educators Association International, "A Professional Association for Christians in Public and Private Schools," http://www.ceai.org/.

7. Alisa Harris, "Getting Religion," *World* 24, no. 23 (November 21, 2009), http://www.worldmag.com/articles/16090.

8. Rudolf Steiner, "Man as Symphony of the Creative Word. Lecture VIII. Rudolf Steiner Archive," November 3, 1923, http://wn.rsarchive.org/Lectures/ManSymphony/19231103p01.html.

9. Joe Nathan, "Charters "Yes!" Vouchers "No!" *Educational Horizons* 83, no. 2 (2005): 110–24.

10. Debra Snell, "Welcome from PLANS President," People for Legal and Nonsectarian Schools (PLANS), http://www.waldorfcritics.org/.

11. Stephanie Saul, "Charter Schools Tied to Turkey Grow in Texas," *New York Times*, June 6, 2011.

12. Rita M. Solnet, "Florida Vouchers: Is This Choice?" Huffington Post, May 18, 2014, www.huffingtonpost.com/rita-m-solnet/florida-vouchers-this-is-_b_4980612.html

13. Americans United for the Separation of Church and State, "D.C. Voucher Program Has Failed to Yield Positive Results, Americans United Tells Senate Committee," www.au.org/media/press-releases/dc-voucher-program-has-failed-to-yield-positive-results-au-tells-senate.

14. Kathleen McGrory, "State: Voucher Proponents Needed to Register as Lobbyists," *Miami Herald*, March 17, 2014.

15. Robert W. Howard, Marvin W. Berkowitz, and Esther F. Schaeffer, "Politics of Character Education," *Educational Policy* 18, no. 1 (2004): 188–215.

16. Howard Kirschenbaum, "A Comprehensive Model for Values Education and Moral Education," *Phi Delta Kappan* 73, no. 10 (1992): 771–76.

17. William Jefferson Clinton's Fourth State of the Union Address, January 23, 1996.

18. "Character Education Crucial to Education System, Paige Says," Department of Education, Archived Information, October 16, 2003, http://www.ed.gov/news/pressreleases/2003/10/10162003.html.

19. The White House, National Character Counts! Week, http://georgewbush-whitehouse.archives.gov/news/releases/2001/10/20011023-23.html.

20. Josephson Institute Center for Youth Ethics. Character Counts! November 30, 2008, http://charactercounts.org/pdf/reportcard/2008/press-release.pdf.

21. Alfie Kohn, "How Not to Teach Values: A Critical Look at Character Education," *Phi Delta Kappan* 78, no. 6 (1997): 428–39.

22. Heather L. Weaver, "Buddist Student, Religious Liberty Prevail in Louisiana," American Civil Liberties Union, March 14, 2014, https://www.aclu.org/blog/religion-belief/buddhist-student-religious-liberty-prevail-louisiana.

# *Chapter Five*

# Vanishing Professions—Teachers and School Leaders

> The people in the government agencies [Finland] running them, from national officials to local authorities, are educators, not business people, military leaders or career politicians.
>
> —Lynnell Hancock[1]

## DEPROFESSIONALIZATION

> In other words, NCLB gives the green light to states that want to lower barriers to the teaching profession.
>
> —Rod Paige, former Secretary of Education[2]

Many powerful individuals from business, political science, public policy, and the military are churned out as the new education bosses. Why would those who do not have college education degrees and/or teaching experience do better educating America's students and leading their schools than real educators? The first area of concern is with teachers.

The deprofessionalizing of teachers escalated with the Department of Education's 2003 report in No Child Left Behind titled *Meeting the Highly Qualified Teachers Challenge*. The report attacked the Colleges of Education for turning out poor teachers, and it called for rigor. Instead of extensive teaching pedagogy, methodology, and practicums, future teachers were to receive supervised practical classroom experiences.

The report also called for alternative teachers to be given a fast track to the classroom through unconventional certification. Performance pay based on test scores became a controversial replacement idea for teacher compensation. Overall, the report ridiculed the teaching profession as needing a complete overall.

But fixing it involved deregulation and placing teachers with less, not more, intensive preparation into the classroom. This provided a boost to a group of college recruits who never studied teaching pedagogy but who had been placed into disadvantaged schools due to a supposed teacher shortage a decade earlier.

## TEACH FOR AMERICA

> The teachers of this country, one may say, have its future in their hands.
>
> —William James, psychologist and philosopher

In 1990, Teach for America (TFA) began sending bachelor-degreed students from elite colleges with five weeks of training into needy schools. Ivy Leaguer Wendy Kopp, herself never a teacher, presented the TFA idea in her thesis. Her idea, based on the Peace Corps and designed to solve a questionable teacher shortage, later became a rallying cry for the group to prove they were a cheaper, more economically savvy way to make teachers.

TFA has become so accepted and the organization so bold that graduates with degrees in any subject—business, gender studies, literature, and others, are becoming certified to teach in areas normally requiring a teacher with specialized preparation. In Idaho, teachers with miniscule preparation in special education can teach students with autism (Cavener, 2013).

Some who join TFA later become real teachers, but usually recruits spend two years in the classroom and move into powerful education administrative positions. Many become state education commissioners, while some start charter schools. Often, they oversee degreed and legitimately licensed teachers, and they may work to close schools and displace those with real teaching degrees. The implication is real degreed and experienced teachers cannot do the job so TFA will. It is also a way to break the teachers unions and replace real educators with cheaper workers.

Kopp has traveled the country cheering TFA and lecturing about educational equity. She receives accolades, brandishing honorary degrees from colleges and universities and kudos from *Business Week*, *Fortune Magazine*, and *U.S. News and World Report*, to name a few. Many look to Kopp as an educational expert despite her lacking education credentials. The mainstream media lavishes unwarranted praise on this group of novices.

Sometimes the group is criticized. In 2007, Canadian columnist, author, and lecturer Heather Mallick, in reference to remarks Kopp made about TFA on *The Colbert Report*, said:

> Things are so bad in that weird private-affluence-and-public-squalor nation that they're allowing a bunch of unqualified college kids—no, they are not teachers in any sense of the word—into classrooms so that school boards don't have to hire actual teachers paid for by the citizenry. I don't mean Appalachia, I mean Washington, D.C. Call me naïve but I was shocked. So was Colbert, who asked, "Why do we need Teach for America if we have No Child Left Behind?" but that was a very Canadian question, I thought, and it clearly mystified Kopp, who has devoted her life to fixing the symptoms of a problem without understanding its roots. She has prominently been made the face of educational reform.[3]

TFA raises private contributions. Corporations, foundations, and celebrities contribute. They also receive funding from local, state, and the federal government (Teach for America, Donors). The long list of corporate funding giants includes Goldman Sachs, the Gap, Google, and a host of other groups. Even the United Negro College Fund rallies behind TFA.

In 2008, the *New York Times*, in "2 School Entrepreneurs Lead the Way on Change," describes how Kopp and her husband, KIPP charter schools' CEO Richard Barth, raised $5.5 million in one night, bringing in corporate executives at the Waldorf-Astoria Hotel in New York (Dillon). Limousines jammed Park Avenue for blocks, and the money raised boosted the $125 million already in the organization's coffers at the time.

TFA proves an attractive alternative for college graduates hungry for jobs that do not exist. A stint with TFA is highlighted on a student's resume and might lead to being hired in another job. In 2012, the TFA website bragged, "At 55 schools—including the University of North Carolina-Chapel Hill, the University of California-Berkeley, Howard University, Yale University, Arizona State University, and Washington University in St. Louis—Teach for America is the top employer of graduating seniors."[4]

School districts fund TFA salaries through contractual agreements, and recruits are usually paid like beginning teachers. This makes TFA attractive to principals managing sparse budgets. It is a salary savings compared to paying career teachers—especially those more experienced at the top of the career ladder.

TFA recruits also get benefits. Unlike most career teachers, they are members of Americorps and can receive $5,730 after each year of teaching, and this can be applied toward loan repayment or for additional expenses in most colleges or universities (Teach for America, Americorps Benefits). Some colleges and universities match these funds. TFA recruits are also permitted to postpone loan payments for a two-year commitment in the classroom.

Tenure, a teacher's right to due process, has been under attack for years, along with the unions that fight for it. If a teacher cannot be fired due to tenure, they could lose their jobs when schools close and they are made to reapply. Instead of a principal rehiring a real teacher, TFA provides the replacement. After two to three years, those from TFA usually leave and another is hired. This assures a constant turnover of young teachers who never rise above the lower salary of a beginning teacher level. They also never gain experience.

Over a six-year period, Stanford University researchers studied certified teachers compared with those from TFA with five weeks of training. By comparing fourth- and fifth-grade reading and math achievement scores from classes between the two groups, they determined that teacher effectiveness was strongly related to teaching preparation (Darling-Hammond et al., 2005). The more prepared one is to teach (i.e., college degreed and area certified), the better teachers performed.

Students taught by traditional teachers made larger gains. TFA did almost as well after receiving teacher certification, and they did better than substitutes in real teacher shortages. But the instability of TFA proves troublesome for poor students who need career teachers committed to teaching long term.

Despite what many TFA advocates claim, and what the media often reports, TFA has not been found to be superior to traditional teachers. Research in favor of the group is often flawed. For example, the 2004 Mathematica Policy Research Study encouraged claims that students taught by TFA recruits did slightly better than other teachers in math and had similar reading results. But a closer look at the study found it compared TFA with those who also had no education degrees or certification.

Many fear that TFA steals jobs from qualified, education-degreed career teachers. In 2007, the Minnesota Association of Colleges for Teacher Education reported a *surplus* of fully licensed career teachers for Minnesota schools. Despite teacher saturation, the State of Minnesota welcomed TFA, claiming a need for diversity.

But colleges already emphasized teacher diversity through the Collaborative Urban Educator (CUE Grant), and the real job needs in areas such as special education and science would not have been filled by TFA. By contracting with Teach for America, Minnesota set up their real teaching candidates to compete with an outside group. The media blamed teachers unions for fighting against TFA and for not allowing the young, inexperienced teachers to get jobs. Minnesota's well-respected credentialing program was changed in 2014 when the University of Minnesota created an alternative teacher-licensing program for TFA supported by the state teaching board (Magan, 2015).

Journalist Barbara Miner of *Rethinking Schools* described the developing split between schools of education and TFA over jobs for new teachers (2010). For example, the University of Illinois graduated about three hundred fully prepared, licensed teachers per year, primarily elementary teachers, who could not find jobs in Chicago schools. Still, cities committed to TFA with lucrative contracts promising recruits for school positions. Dallas added one hundred TFA recruits after 350 teachers were laid off, and Boston's school district replaced twenty veteran teachers with TFA recruits.

In 2009, North Carolina's Charlotte-Mecklenburg school district dismissed hundreds of licensed veteran teachers citing low performance evaluations, but exempted TFA recruits (Sawchuk, 2009). In almost every urban school district, TFA replaces career teachers. Ironically, college-degreed and credentialed teachers are often necessary to assist TFA recruits in the classroom. They are necessary mentors.

Programs such as Teach for America would be better as Teacher Assistants for America. Graduates could work in classrooms under the tutelage of real teachers. If, after working with education-degreed and authentically credentialed teachers, those from TFA decided to become real teachers, they could return to college to get a master's degree in teaching.

But this is not the purpose of the program. TFA recruits are trained to see themselves as *real* teachers. By taking over classrooms and pushing real teachers out of jobs, TFA continues to degrade the teaching profession. Long term, this could end professional teaching as we know it.

While some TFA alumni have gone on to high-caliber jobs in education, others have written troubling exposés of their years involved with the program. In 2014, students on various college campuses across the country from

United Students Against Sweatshops drew attention to TFA's poor recruitment and training practices (Hing, 2014). The students called for TFA to only send its recruits into places with *real* teacher shortages and that they get more than five weeks of training. They also asked TFA to end their corporate partnerships.

## THE NEW TEACHER PROJECT

> Monday, the school board is expected to approve a $1 million payment of Gates money to TNTP, the first of two installments totaling $2.5 million this year.
>
> —Jane Roberts[5]

Along with Teach for America, school districts across the country increasingly rely on other groups of alternative teachers. Such teachers used to be rare, hired only when principals could not find credentialed teachers. With less preparation and understanding of child development, the job is often difficult.

Michelle Rhee, who came from Teach for America and was former chancellor of Washington, DC schools, is a well-known critic of teachers. She promoted The New Teacher Project (TNTP), a nonprofit organization run mostly by those from TFA. When TNTP contracts with a school district, they get immense power in hiring decisions (The New Teacher Project, Our Clients). The organization slights professionally prepared teachers since a large part of the purpose of TNTP is to do their own teacher training.

TNTP has published several reports criticizing the evaluation process of teachers, including "The Widget Effect: Our National Failure to Acknowledge and Act on Differences in Teacher Effectiveness." The report claims teacher effectiveness is the most important quality for student achievement (Weisberg et al., 2009). Education Secretary Arne Duncan (never a teacher himself) praised the report.

In 2010, TNTP, using the Widget report and the Washington, DC IMPACT Study (instituted under Rhee), claimed older teacher evaluations were flawed. But Richard H. Milner IV, associate professor of education at Vanderbilt University, described flaws in the report itself, claiming nothing unique was found. It seemed designed to create suspicion of teachers and their evaluation system.

Good schools have always provided decent teacher evaluations. Well-prepared principals review lesson plans, make impromptu visits to classrooms, and schedule teacher observations. Principals, who have worked with children and who supervise teachers, understand how to assess a teacher's performance and can make recommendations for improvement. When principals are engaged in their schools, they are capable of good teacher evaluations.

TNTP, headquartered in New York City, partners with the New York Teaching Fellows, which have changed education policy, making it easier to hire alternative teachers. Depending on where you live, there may also be a religious connection involving teacher preparation. In Memphis, Tennessee, Teaching Fellows are tied to the Memphis Teacher Residency Program, which trains teachers through Union University—a Christian school. Its mission is "to positively impact student achievement in Memphis' urban schools by recruiting, training, and supporting outstanding teachers, all within a Christian context."[6]

TNTP is backed and promoted by the same individuals who contribute to other nonprofit and for-profit privatization school endeavors. TNTP's marketing strategy to undo formal teacher preparation and credentialing is fierce, with publications and self-made reports not only seeking to evaluate teachers differently but also to ultimately eliminate tenure.

In 2008, *Fast Company* described TNTP as one of the "45 Social Entrepreneurs Who Are Changing the World." They stated: "Over the next five years, it intends to realize a fundamental shift in the way quality teachers are generated, trained, and matched to schools."[7] It is easy to see this occurring, but not for positive reasons.

TNTP also promotes the controversial Value-Added Measurement (VAM). VAM originated from the work of William Sanders, a statistician from Tennessee who worked in agriculture. VAM measures how students do year by year on standardized tests, and teachers are judged according to scores. Higher VAM scores credit teachers as succeeding. VAM is highly controversial. Those working with the most difficult or academically challenged students, or those teaching in areas harder to evaluate, could be judged unfairly.

## COLLEGES OF EDUCATION

> If there was any piece of legislation that I could pass it would be to blow up colleges of education.
>
> —Reid Lyon, chief of Child Development Behavior Branch, National Institute of Child Development, NIH[8]

At the heart of current attempts to dismantle professional teaching is whether Colleges of Education (COE) degrees matter. Those who have never earned teaching degrees, or worked in schools, are often the loudest critics.

In 2009, a reporter for the *Wall Street Journal*, discussing an interview with public school critic and businessman Eli Broad, noted, "Mr. Broad tells me in no uncertain terms that it is time to get rid of education schools—'they're the lowest ranking students at a university.'"[9] Such pronouncements have been perpetuated repeatedly by the media and go a long way toward damaging COE programs. It also discourages bright, motivated young people from going into teaching as a real career and promotes a short-term TFA experience.

Critics of COEs support a business approach to managing public schools. Long-term, formal teacher preparation and credentialing does not seem to matter (Finn and Madigan, 2001). In their eyes, anyone with a degree can teach. Education researcher David Berliner, considering such criticisms, states, "The vast majority of those who bash the entire system of teacher education are ill-informed, unhappy about other aspects of education in America, or cheap."[10]

What does it involve to become a teacher through the COE? Most university teacher preparation involves coursework in the liberal arts at the start. Later, teachers specialize in the area they will be teaching. Courses can include child development, teaching in urban settings, teaching mathematics, reading, social studies, and literacy. Assessment, communication, and technology might also be a part of teacher preparation. In some colleges, the costly and controversial edTPA, connected to the National Board for Professional Teaching Standards and Pearson, is used.

COE-degreed future teachers might take additional coursework in special and bilingual education in order to teach children with special needs. This could include areas such as autism; gifted and talented; developmentally disabled; emotional and/or learning disabled; and multicultural children. Education colleges could also address the uniqueness of middle school (grades six through eight) and preadolescence.

At Arizona State University, secondary teachers preparing to teach grades seven to twelve focus on coursework in subjects they wish to teach by following a subject map—that is, English, history, social studies, mathematics, earth science, and more. The iteachAZ program is well respected by principals in Arizona. Students also learn about diversity, cultures, and a variety of other issues pertaining to adolescent development, literacy, critical issues, and methods.

All COE programs send teachers into the field to student teach under the supervision of career-credentialed, degreed teachers. Some programs include a practicum in which students get additional supervised experience teaching children. Such long-term coursework and experience are usually missing with TFA and alternative teaching programs. While no one argues education schools cannot improve, eliminating quality teacher preparation programs altogether is a serious matter. It will be the end of a profession that has great value to society and its children.

In some states, alternative collegelike programs to create teachers who focus more on high-stakes testing and strict teaching are being created to compete or replace COEs. One of the most recognized groups is the Relay Graduate School of Education, which offers master's degrees to teachers and also leadership training for principals. But this mostly online group is all about reform, and the founders come from a charter school network including Uncommon Schools, KIPP, and Achievement First (Relay GSE).

## TEACHER CERTIFICATION

> Success depends upon previous preparation, and without such preparation there is sure to be failure.
>
> —Confucius

> There is no shortcut to achievement. Life requires thorough preparation—veneer isn't worth anything.
>
> —George Washington Carver

Questions have been raised as to the relevance of the teacher education accreditation process administered through the National Council for Accreditation of Teacher Education (NCATE). Much of the criticism revolves around attempts to lower teacher requirements. The NCATE demands strict preparation of teachers who pursue scholarly study in COEs. At the same time, they partner with state education departments who relax requirements for teacher certification for those with minimal preparation in programs such as Teach for America and other alternative programs. NCATE has not used its muscle to dissuade state partners from fast-track preparation of teachers (Johnson, Johnson, Farenga, and Ness, 2005, 73).

Educational researchers Laczko-Kerr and Berliner determined that traditionally certified teachers "significantly outperformed" teachers who were "undercertified."[11]

Those who sign up for speedy online teacher preparation programs are also able to quickly become credentialed under questionable validation procedures. State certification, reserved in the past for those who completed a teacher education program in a particular area along with student teaching, has been consistently devalued.

A degree in special education, for example, once prepared teachers to teach in a special needs area only through appropriate certification. Schools initiated temporary allowances if a certified teacher could not be found, but serious attempts were made to find a teacher with appropriate credentials. This validation process provided parents with assurance that teachers had matching credentials for the subject taught. Now that is changing.

The American Board for Certification of Teacher Excellence (ABCTE) advertises helping teachers get their teaching degree and credentials in ten months. They call it "Teacher Certification to Fit Your Busy Life."[12] ABCTE is a nonprofit organization funded by the federal government for $5 million in September 2001. As of 2014, Florida, Idaho, Mississippi, Missouri, New Hampshire, Nevada, Oklahoma, Pennsylvania, South Carolina, Tennessee, Utah, and other locations approved of teachers certified through ABCTE. The current cost to become quickly certified in an ABCTE, including the online program, is $2,020.[13] ABCTE is supported and directed by education reformers. But in some areas, the Chamber of Commerce diminishes the importance of state certification regulations.

The Department of Education (DOE) touts "highly qualified" teachers and includes the ABCTE program. But this program encourages individuals to bypass real degrees from legitimate colleges. The 2003 newsletter, *DOE Education Innovator* #20, states: "This year a new teacher certification process will be launched that will help states, districts, and communities meet the requirements of *No Child Left Behind* by credentialing prospective teachers and providing advanced credentialing for experienced teachers."[14]

If certification "light" seems hard to fathom, sometimes teachers have *no* certification when they begin teaching. Federal law allowing individuals from alternative programs to teach while seeking certification (they do this all the time with TFA) drew protest from California parents, students, and community organizations (Honawar, 2007).

In *Renee v. Spellings, Dist. Court, ND California*, plaintiffs asserted "a teacher-in-training with no prior training and no prior teaching experience may be deemed 'highly qualified' the very day he or she enters an 'alternative certification program' and begin to serve as a classroom teacher."[15]

Such teachers, they pointed out, wind up in "lower-performing" schools with "students of color." But the court ruled against the plaintiffs, contending "Congress created these 'alternative route' programs to help local school districts in high-poverty and high-need areas meet their teaching goals by enabling them to recruit capable individuals who had not completed teacher preparation programs and quickly enable those individuals to become teachers in high-need schools."[16]

California, like other states, had an abundance of college-credentialed English teachers, yet nonuniversity certification programs dominated certification (Baines, 2006). English teachers come from online programs offered by for-profit colleges such as National Louis University, University of Phoenix, Walden University, and others. Graduates from established programs, such as UCLA, sent fewer teachers into the field.

Credentialing teachers includes private partnerships and deregulation and accelerated programs with little oversight. More research is called for involving the credentialing process, but, in the meantime, parents should demand to know a teacher's credentials. They should not take it for granted that the teacher teaching their child is qualified. Teachers should make degrees and certificates of recognition visible in their classrooms. And school PTAs should provide parents a list of teacher credentials.

## NATIONAL COUNCIL ON TEACHER QUALITY

Many education critics are now so embedded in public schooling it is difficult to determine the validity of what Americans hear or read. In 2013, a controversial report by the Washington-based National Council on Teacher Quality (NCTQ) was published, along with the *U.S. News and World Report* state-by-state rankings of schools of education. The picture was not pretty. Education schools received an F. But looking deeper into the report, one finds it comes from a group with a preconceived agenda. The Thomas B. Fordham Foundation created the NCTQ in 2000 (2002).

The NCTQ Board of Directors includes at this time many individuals supportive of privatization. Chester E. Finn Jr., for example, was once connected to Edison Schools and is currently senior fellow and president emeritus of the Thomas B. Fordham Institute. He was assistant education secretary in President Reagan's administration. Another example is Kate Walsh, who worked for the Abell Foundation in Baltimore, the Baltimore City Public Schools, and with Core Knowledge Foundation. She has supported school privatization for years.

Others on the advisory board include: Sir Michael Barber, chief education advisor, Pearson International; Michael Feinburg, KIPP founder; Eric A. Hanushek from the Hoover Institution; and Joel I. Klein, the one-time controversial chancellor of New York. Wendy Kopp, creator of Teach for America, also sits on the advisory board. Since Kopp's TFA organization stands to win more contracts with the destruction of the Colleges of Education, this would appear to be a conflict of interest. Contributors to NCTQ include the Bill and Melinda Gates Foundation, the Broad Foundation, and many others.

Longtime dean of the Indiana University School of Education, Gerardo M. Gonzalez, defended their teacher education program, stating, "The report issued today, June 18, by the National Council on Teacher Quality, in conjunction with *U.S. News and World Report*, is not based on accepted means of program evaluation or examination of actual program outcomes. IU School of Education graduates are performing at the highest levels and making a difference in the classroom."[17]

Linda Darling-Hammond, chair of the California Commission on Teacher Credentialing and the Charles E. Ducommun Professor of Education at Stanford University, responded in the *Washington Post*'s The Answer Sheet that the report "published badly flawed information without the fundamental concerns for accuracy that any serious research enterprise would insist upon."[18]

Dean Donald Heller from Michigan State University said:

> Objections have focused largely on the methodology used by NCTQ, which revolves mostly around a review of syllabi and other teaching materials from courses in teacher preparation programs. There have also been criticisms of the coercive nature of the study; NCTQ did not invite institutions to participate, but instead forced them to by utilizing lawsuits and Freedom of Information Act requests to gain access to the materials at public colleges and universities that refused to provide them voluntarily. Others have pointed to the perception that NCTQ, largely because of funding it has received from some foundations deemed to be politically conservative, has a particular agenda it is pursu-

ing. That agenda is to shut down traditional teacher preparation programs in favor of alternative certification programs, such as Teach for America.[19]

The NCTQ provides no realistic way of improving public schools, is a waste of manpower, and is deceptive to the public. But destroying public schooling does not only involve deregulating the teaching profession, it also includes changing how principals are prepared.

## NEW LEADERS

The role of principal is critical to the smooth running and day-to-day operation of a school. In 2001, Harvard Business School's *Social Enterprise* described the winners of their Business Plan Contest—a program to make alternative public school principals (2001). New Leaders for New Schools, changed to New Leaders (NL), is to principals what Teach for America is to teachers.

Jonathan Schnur is the main creator of NL. The principal residents receive salaries and are considered a part of the school administration, acting as assistant principals or principals—jobs that used to be reserved for those prepared through years of classroom teaching experience and college coursework in educational administration. NL recruits come from many fields and often without knowledge about and experience working with children.

Like Wendy Kopp, I could find no education degree or child-centered experience for NL founder Jonathan Schnur. He has a BA degree from Princeton—like Kopp. His background is in politics, but he worked as a special assistant to Secretary of Education Richard Riley and as President Clinton's White House associate director for educational policy. He was a senior advisor on education to Vice President Gore, and he developed national educational policies concerning teacher and principal quality by working on issues such as after-school programs, school district reform, charter schools, and preschools (Center for American Progress).

During his time with the Clinton administration, Schnur visited many schools. But visiting schools and studying and working as a credentialed educator are different experiences. Without formal preparation in education, or experience working with children, it is a mystery how Schnur became an authority on public schools and the needs of children.

Schnur worked as campaign advisor to President Barack Obama, and he played a critical role in writing the president's school stimulus plan (Green,

2009). Some thought the president would choose him to be education secretary or chief of staff to Secretary of Education Arne Duncan, but that did not occur. He returned to working with New Leaders.

Like TFA, NL claims the ability to transform schools. The implication is that alternatively trained individuals will do this in a way no degreed, administratively prepared, and experienced principal could ever do. No research shows this to be true.

Part of the Obama administration's stimulus package goes toward NL training, and cities across the country subscribe to the program. In 2009, for example, the financially strapped Memphis City School Board announced the approval of a $3.2 million contract with NL to help create high school principals (Roberts, 2009). It would seem to make more sense to fund ways of better preparing principals in university education schools.

NL, like TFA, is backed by wealthy donors and corporations. Eli Broad called NL a "model for the nation" in 2001, before the program got off the ground.[20] The Los Angeles–based Broad Foundation partnered with Chicago Public Schools, providing $1.2 million dollars for NL at that time.

In 2004, Schnur, on NPR, likened turning around a failed school to "leading an Army unit into Iraq."[21] His initiative on the program was to encourage the recruiting of principals, especially military colonels, to lead public schools. But it could be argued that public schools never had a crisis with principals and leadership.

Jonathan Schnur was the keynote speaker at the 2010 Stanford Business of Education Symposium. He became the cofounder of America Achieves, another group advocating college preparation for all children. He sits on the board of Opportunity Nation, a bipartisan campaign stressing the need to close America's opportunity gap. Opportunity Nation is connected to Be the Change, Inc., run by KIPP leader Richard Barth, who is Teach for America creator Wendy Kopp's husband.

## SUPERINTENDENTS AND SCHOOL LEADERS

Like teachers and principals, two different ideologies are at play in the role of superintendents and school leaders. Traditionally, school administrators moved through the ranks as teachers and principals and obtained educational administration degrees before becoming leaders. Many got doctorates. But changes have been made as to who will be hired in such positions. Many local and state superintendents and educational leaders are hired in positions without education credentials. This is a different from the past.

In educational leadership programs, teachers have usually studied coursework leading to master's degrees or to a PhD. The requirements can include a combination of coursework, depending on the kind of leadership sought. Policy studies, school development, education history, politics, economics, culture, organization, leadership methods, and research are all courses worth study. Other coursework might include school funding and finance, curriculum and instruction, legal aspects involving education, teacher leadership, and personnel administration.

Education reformers insist nontraditional superintendents only require passion about the kind of business reform best to forward school privatization initiatives. They encourage those from business, law, and the military to consider a job in education. If individuals want a principal or educational administration position, they can apply to the Eli Broad Superintendents Academy, started in 2002. The Broad curriculum heavily emphasizes standards, test scores, and stakeholder engagement.

Those who graduate from the Broad program infiltrate urban public schools with a privatization agenda. The emphasis is on closing traditional public schools in favor of charter schools. In a space of two weeks, teachers at Central Falls High School in Central Falls, Rhode Island, a heavily Hispanic school overseen at that time by State Education Commissioner Deborah Gist, were fired; Kansas City superintendent John Covington shut down half the schools there; and numerous public schools were threatened with closure in Detroit by Financial Director Robert Bobb. What did each administrator have in common? They all graduated from Eli Broad's Superintendents Academy.

Not every school leader is required to get training. A partial list of nontraditional superintendents includes: former US attorney Alan Bersin, who directed San Diego's schools and later became California's education leader; Citibank executive Harold Levy, who became New York City's schools chancellor; US Assistant Attorney General Joel Klein, who followed Levy; and Chicago superintendent Paul Vallas, who was originally the city budget director (Helfand and Nicholas, 2005). Vallas moved to lead Philadelphia schools and eventually took over the mostly chartered school system in New Orleans. Later he became superintendent of Bridgeport, Connecticut schools and eventually left that position to get into politics.

Bersin, "hired to shake up San Diego schools," was accused of implementing "heavy-handed education policies," but he garnered praise among national education reformers.[22] Former Governor Arnold Schwarzenegger moved Bersin into California's top educational role. Later, President Obama tapped him to be commissioner of US Customs and Border Protection, a role he had held previously under President Clinton. Levy became the last school board *elected* chancellor in New York City.

In 2010, Education Chancellor Joel Klein, after implementing many contentious school reforms in New York City, left to work in Rupert Murdoch's News Corporation. News Corporation was described by the *Wall Street Journal* as "one of the biggest players in the increasingly crowded field of corporate investors chasing the next technology to transform American education."[23] The program fell apart in 2015. Former mayor Michael Bloomberg quickly replaced Klein with Cathie Black, former Hearst Magazines executive and former publisher of *USA Today*. But many called for Black to step down due to her lack of experience, and she was replaced.

Mayors appoint many urban superintendents. The democratic superintendent selection process, through an elected school board, is obstructed when this occurs, and the process opens the door to privatization. Perhaps the best-known appointed school chancellor is past Teach for America recruit Michelle Rhee.

## MICHELLE RHEE

In 2007, newly elected Washington, DC, mayor Adrian M. Fenty (D) greased the school privatization wheels. In one of his first moves, he ousted Superintendent Clifford Janey and appointed as chancellor Teach for America recruit and New Teacher Project facilitator Michelle Rhee. Although many in DC criticized Janey's ousting (he had only been superintendent for three years), they praised Fenty's selection of Rhee.

Choosing a TFA recruit over a qualified education leader proved a bold move, and a new day for privatization enthusiasts. Accolades came from high-level education reformers. Education Secretary Margaret Spellings and New York City Chancellor Joel Klein praised the selection. The media gave short shrift to Rhee's slim resume and seemed not to care that her few references (Laura Bush the exception) came from individuals with nonschool backgrounds.

Even George Parker, the teachers union president, given little say in the selection process, reassured everyone, saying, "In meeting with her, I left with a sense of optimism that Ms. Rhee has the capacity to get the job done, that she is collaborative. . . . I left there feeling like she gets it, she really gets it."[24] Parker would eventually go to work for Michelle Rhee's Students First program.

Rhee lacked any education degree, but her resume boasted three years of teaching in a Baltimore public-private partnership school run by Education Alternatives, Inc. No one could prove Rhee's claim of raising test scores from the thirteenth to the ninetieth percentile within two years (coworkers vouched for her).

But *Washington Post* columnist Jay Matthews said of Rhee, "She is the first of their generation of educational innovators named to head a major school system and symbol of their efforts to help inner-city children and challenge the power of education schools, teachers unions and the many layers of central offices that often smother creativity."[25]

In reality, Rhee's classroom practices were anything but dull. In a 2007 *TIME* interview, she discussed her Teach for America stint that took place in 1993. Her students were "more out of control than ever," and to capture their attention she swatted a bumblebee when it landed on her desk and she "popped it into her mouth and gulped it down."[26]

Serious concerns were also raised later when a video began circulating on the Internet of Rhee bragging and laughing about taping her students' mouths shut while escorting them to lunch. She describes, in a jolly manner, how the tape hurt the children and how when the tape was pulled off, their mouths bled (Kugler, 2010). The *Washington Post* verified the video was real.

Rhee's classroom management difficulties, however, would later engender little compassion for problems facing DC teachers. She fired many of them, even though her time in the classroom appeared to be nothing outstanding, and she had experienced her own struggles. If teachers thought they would get an understanding classroom comrade, they were disappointed. Rhee followed a "do as I say, and not as I do" formula.

Rhee's six-figure salary, and the high salaries going to many young workers on her staff, caused controversy, but in the end the City Council rationalized the salaries, claiming they needed the very best talent. One could not help but wonder how little formal teaching education, or adequate long-term experience, adequately defined *best*.

Rhee surrounded herself with young nonprofit strategists (Labbe, 2007). She made no secret that the private sector figured prominently in her plans. She favored school closings and takeovers in the form of charter schools. She spoke incessantly about going after the city's so-called failing high schools (Mills, 2008). And she tied teacher evaluations to student test scores in a program called IMPACT. She garnered support from the Broad and Gates foundations and other school reformers.

Rhee started her reign by firing 121 employees, including thirty-six principals, and even the principal at her daughter's school. In a 2007 PBS report, John Merrow asked Rhee if she had compassion when firing principals. She answered: "Compassion? I think that when you're doing the kind of work that I'm doing in public education, where the lives and futures of children hang in the balance, you can't play with that."[27] When Merrow questioned whether the school district was a democracy, she replied: "We're not going to make every decision within this district by taking a hand count."[28]

In what appeared to be a way to rid the system of career teachers, Rhee proposed a $100,000 buyout plan of older teachers. In the deal, teachers would get a salary increase by giving up tenure. With Teach for America and the New Teacher Project working to provide replacements, Rhee would have little trouble filling vacated positions after ridding the district of teachers, and her actions met the approval of privatization fans.

In 2009, educators thought President Obama might pick a traditional education leader as Secretary of Education. Stanford professor Linda Darling-Hammond, with a rich education background, had advised the president on his campaign and seemed a likely pick. Immediately, right-wing and left-wing articles and education blogs denounced Darling-Hammond's choice.

At the same time, Rhee's picture holding a broom appeared on the cover of *TIME*, and the featured article titled "Can She Save Our Schools?" referred to Rhee. Supporters interpreted Rhee's broom as a symbol of her sweeping away problems in DC schools. Critics saw the picture differently. Rhee's name surfaced as a candidate for education secretary, but Arne Duncan was ultimately chosen for the position.

Perhaps the most caustic display of Rhee's power overload occurred in 2009 when 266 teachers and staff were removed from their classrooms. Rhee's march to rid the district of teachers became more than the usual pink slip. Claudia Ricci, a journalism student at Georgetown University, expressed astonishment at what little media coverage occurred as teachers were marched from their schools. According to Ricci:

> My friend described the scene. It was just minutes before the bell rang. No one knew it was coming. The doors of certain classrooms opened. Armed policemen wearing bullet-proof vests appeared. Accompanying the cops were the new teachers who informed the existing teachers that they had been replaced. No warning at all.[29]

It did not end with the jolting of teachers from their classrooms while startled children watched. In a *Fast Company* interview months later, Rhee, while asked about the union's accusation that she "budget crunched numbers" to fire teachers and staff, replied "I got rid of teachers who had hit children, who had had sex with children, who had missed 78 days of school."[30] The outcry by horrified parents and educators appeared to put Rhee in the hot seat. But by June 2010, Rhee negotiated a new teacher contract dumping seniority, tenure, and installing performance pay.

The *Washington Post*'s Bill Turque, who consistently reviewed Rhee's tactics, described how she at one point advised New York City chancellor Joel Klein concerning contracts and how *New York Daily News* publisher Mort Zuckerman placed a "dueling" op-ed between union leader Randi Weingarten and Rhee. Turque noted that Zuckerman had "ponied up big money to support New York City Chancellor Joel Klein" and that Klein, Rhee, and Zuckerman sat "on the board of the Broad Center for the Management of School Systems, which trains and recruits executive talent to run urban districts. Broad's philanthropic arm also helped fund Rhee's performance pay plan."[31]

In 2010, Mayor Fenty's ousting by voters meant the end of Rhee's DC reign. She quickly blamed the union for their ejection but continued to exert influence, and she received lavish media praise. At a 2010 education event, then *NBC's Meet the Press* commentator David Gregory gushed:

> Before we begin, we have Chancellor Michelle Rhee here, and I just want to say publicly what I say privately, which is, thank you for what you've done, thank you for your commitment, for your leadership, for your stick-to-it-ness and for the result that you have achieved. Washington, D.C. will miss you greatly. . . . But your commitment to kids and to education endures and there will be a great many people lining up to support you and your efforts.[32]

After Rhee's removal as DC chancellor, the *Wall Street Journal* announced: "Ms. Rhee said her group will develop an aggressive legislative agenda for state leaders and local school districts that will include tying student test scores to teacher tenure decisions and lifting the cap on charter schools, public schools run by outside groups. 'This will not be for the faint of heart,' she said."[33] And also the *Wall Street Journal* noted that Rhee announced on *Oprah*, "I am going to start a revolution."[34]

In 2011, questions surfaced about possible cheating violations on tests during Rhee's DC years as chancellor (Gillum and Bello). The Office of the State Superintendent of Education and the Caveon Consulting Firm investigated eight schools, and only one school was found to have high erasure rates due to a teacher's mistake. But the investigation did not seem complete, and the demands of Rhee were only slight.

In a strange turn of events, education journalist John Merrow described how he knew about the cheating due to a missing memo he learned about that indicated more schools and teachers were involved in the cheating than originally thought (2013).

Merrow goes so far as to revisit and question his own *PBS Frontline* interview with Rhee. But the cheating incident, while still in the minds of many, seemed to get little real attention, and the plight of the DC school system is no better off since her reign. Rhee forged ahead with her organization Students First, whose initiatives pushed privatization. In 2014, she announced she would be stepping down as the CEO.

## SECRETARY OF EDUCATION

Secretaries of Education deal with education issues from early education through college. Only one education secretary actually taught children. President Reagan appointed a high school teacher, Terrel H. Bell, to the position. Bell established the National Commission on Excellence in Education.

The 1983 report *A Nation at Risk: The Imperative for Educational Reform* resulted from that commission. Despite negative publicity against public schools, generated by neoconservatives in the Reagan administration, Bell supported public schools and eventually resigned in disagreement over school spending cuts.

William Bennett (1985–1988) became Bell's replacement. Bennett cast public schools as failing while supporting a privatization agenda. He can still be found promoting Common Core State Standards and Next Generation Science, and he helped start the online program K12 Inc.

President H. W. Bush selected Lauro F. Cavazos (1989–1990), a college dean with a background in zoology and physiology to be education secretary, and Senator Lamar Alexander (1990–1993), whose background was in law, would follow. President Clinton chose Richard W. Riley, a politician, to be his education secretary.

President George W. Bush's first education secretary, Rod Paige (2001–2005), a coach, college administrator, school board member, and superintendent of the Houston Independent School District, called the National Education Association a "terrorist organization" because they refused to support his standards agenda.[35] Margaret Spellings replaced Paige when he went into private business. Both Paige and Spellings were instrumental in devising and promoting NCLB. They also criticized teachers and promoted alternative teacher credentialing.

In a letter to the chief state school officers in September 2006, Secretary of Education Margaret Spellings said of America's educational system: "To meet the goal that all students will be on grade level in reading and mathematics by 2014, we need to pick up the pace in our efforts to ensure that all core academic subjects are taught by highly qualified and effective teachers."[36]

Never clearly defined, teachers who taught successfully for years were suddenly told they did not have appropriate credentials. It became harder for those with real credentials to get hired but easier if you came from an alternative program.

While discussing the much-maligned term "highly qualified" at an education congressional meeting, Representative Michael M. Honda (D-CA), a former public school teacher and principal, asked Secretary Spellings, "What in your background makes you a highly qualified Secretary of Education?"[37] Spellings replied that she had been a substitute teacher. She had degrees in journalism and political science and enjoyed making policy. In 2015, Spellings became the president of the North Carolina public university system.

In 2009, newly elected President Obama selected Arne Duncan to be Secretary of Education. Duncan, a nontraditional superintendent of Chicago Public Schools, never taught school or led a faculty as principal. He claims as a child he observed his mother tutoring disadvantaged students. Although the media praises Duncan, his controversial tenure as Chicago superintendent and the actions he has taken since (support of charter schools and performance pay) made it clear that privatization was a part of his agenda. Duncan resigned in 2015.

## CONCLUSION: EDUCATORS

Classroom teachers and those in support positions such as librarians, teacher aides, counselors, and school nurses have seen their positions cut. This often occurs when a public school is shuttered in favor of a new charter school. And claims of a teacher shortage continue to grow even though career teachers continue to be devalued. Outright attacks on teachers and their unions weaken the structure of the job description.

One of the best examples of this was when California teachers lost their right to due process after the contentious *Vergara v. State of California* (2014). Millionaire Dave Welch from Silicon Valley, a corporate public relations entrepreneur who started the nonprofit Students Matter, manufactured the lawsuit. The case was filled with questionable accusations, including claims that the 2013 Pasadena Teacher of the Year did not give one of the plaintiffs enough schoolwork. The teacher presented ample proof of her ability to provide good instruction, including her class syllabi.

Expert witnesses such as education researchers David Berliner and Linda Darling-Hammond testified for the defense. But Los Angeles Unified School District's superintendent John Deasy provided a poor argument for the teachers he oversaw. Deasy, once a science teacher, completed training with the Broad Institute. As noted in chapter 6, he abruptly resigned in 2014 over an iPad scandal.

The good news is that teachers find support on social media, making connections with other educators and support groups from around the country—and the world. Through Facebook and Twitter, teachers, principals, and parents are more connected than ever before. The Badass Teachers Association (BATs) also brings professionals and parents together and provides a valuable forum for education activists to have their voices heard.

Every teacher and education administrator should be required to have formal teaching and leadership preparation, and they deserve due process when it comes to job protection. In no other profession would such deregulation be permitted. It is difficult to believe that those who know so little about children have been allowed to dominate teaching and educational leadership positions. This lack of preparedness will continue to be a cause for concern until Americans insist upon fully prepared and authentically credentialed professionals.

## NOTES

1. LynNell Hancock, "Why Are Finland's Schools Successful?" *Smithsonian* 42, no. 5 (2011): 94–102.

2. "Meeting the Highly Qualified Teachers Challenge, The Secretary's Second Annual Report on Teacher Quality," US Department of Education, Office of Postsecondary Education, June 2003, http://www2.ed.gov/about/reports/annual/teachprep/2003title-ii-report.pdf.

3. Heather Mallick, "Basic Education Shouldn't Need Fundraising Drives," Rabble.ca, May 18, 2007, http://rabble.ca/news/basic-education-shouldnt-need-fundraising-drives.

4. "Teach for America to Bring a Record 10,000 Teachers to Nation's Highest-Need Classrooms in 2012," Teach for America, https://www.teachforamerica.org/press-room/press-releases/2012/teach-america-bring-record-10000-teachers-nation's-highest-need-0.

5. Jane Roberts, "Now Hiring," *The Commercial Appeal*, March 14, 2010.

6. Memphis Teacher Residency, Mission, https://memphistr.org/.

7. Fast Company, Social Capitalists: The New Teacher Project, "45 Social Entrepreneurs Who Are Changing the World," http://www.fastcompany.com/social/2008/profiles/new-teacher-project.html.

8. Susan Ohanian, "Terroristic Threats by Bush Education Advisor," *Substance*, January 2003.

9. Naomi Schaefer Riley, "'We're in the Venture Philanthropy Business,'" *Wall Street Journal*, August 28, 2009.

10. David C. Berliner, "A Personal Response to Those Who Bash Teacher Education," *Journal of Teacher Education* 51, no. 5 (2000): 358–71.

11. Ildiko Laczko-Kerr and David C. Berliner, "The Effectiveness of 'Teach for America' and Other Under-Certified Teachers on Student Academic Achievement: A Case of Harmful Public Policy," *Educational Policy Analysis Archives* 19, no. 37 (2002), http://hub.mspnet.org/index.cfm/9399.

12. American Board for Certification of Teacher Excellence, "How to Enroll to Become a Teacher," http://www.abcte.org/teach.

13. Ibid.

14. US Department of Education, "The Education Innovator 20," Achieved Information, July 14, 2003, http://www.ed.gov/news/newsletters/innovator/2003/0714.html.

15. *Renee v. Spellings, Dist. Court, ND California*, June 17, 2008.

16. Ibid.

17. Geraldo M. Gonzalez, "IU School of Education Response to NCTQ Teacher Prep Review," June 18, 2013, IUPUI Newsroom, http://newsinfo.iu.edu/news/page/normal/24345.html.

18. Valerie Strauss, "Why the NCTQ Teacher Prep Ratings Are Nonsense," The Answer Sheet, *Washington Post*, June 18, 2013.

19. Donald Heller, "The Skinny on the NCTQ Teacher Prep Review," Michigan State University, College of Education, June 19, 2013, http://edwp.educ.msu.edu/dean/2013/the-skinny-on-the-nctq-teacher-prep-review/.

20. The Broad Foundation, Education, Press Releases, March 26, 2001, http://broadeducation.org/news/152.html.

21. *The Connection*, Boston NPR, 2004.

22. Maureen Magee, "Bersin's Legacy a Study in Contradiction," *San Diego Union-Tribune*, May 1, 2005.

23. Russell Adams and Jessica E. Vascellaro, "News Corp. Crams for Classes," *Wall Street Journal*, December 13, 2010.

24. Mike DeBonis, "Union Jacked," *Washington City Paper*, July 25, 2007.

25. Jay Matthews, "Maverick Teachers' Key D.C. Moment," *Washington Post*, June 18, 2007.

26. Martha Brant, "Michelle Rhee: Unconventional, Bee Swallowing Reformer," *Newsweek*, December 31, 2007.

27. "Leadership: A Challenging Course. Michelle Rhee in Washington D.C., Episode 2: Facing Expectations," Transcript, November 19, 2007, learningmatters.tv/blog/on-pbs-newshour/michelle-rhee-in-washington-dc-episode-2-facing-expectations/1088/.

28. PBS Newshour, "D.C. Schools Chief Rhee Faces High Hopes for Reform," Transcript, November 19, 2007, http://www.pbs.org/newshour/bb/education-july-dec07-dcschools_11-19/.

29. Claudia Ricci, "Students Watched While DC Police Removed Their Teachers," *Huffington Post*, October 11, 2009, http://www.huffingtonpost.com/claudia-ricci/the-students-watched-whil_b_316859.html.

30. Jeff Chu, "Update: Michelle Rhee vs. the DC Teachers' Union," February 1, 2010, http://www.fastcompany.com/magazine/142/update-dc-report-card.html.

31. Bill Turque, "Weingarten to Rhee: Save the Advice on N.Y.C," *Washington Post*, June 17, 2010.

32. Alan. Suderman, "Warning: Don't Diss *Meet the Press* to David Gregory in a Crowded Ballroom," Washington City Paper.Com Blog, October 28, 2010, http://www.washingtoncitypaper.com/blogs/looselips/2010/10/28/warning-dont-diss-meet-the-press-to-david-gregory-in-a-crowded-ballroom/.

33. Stephanie Banchero, "Michelle Rhee Launches Education Project," *Wall Street Journal*, December 6, 2010.

34. Ibid.

35. Greg Toppo, "Education Chief Calls Teachers 'Terrorist Organization,'" *USA Today*, February 23, 2004.

36. US Department of Education, "Key Policy Letters Signed by the Education Secretary or Deputy Secretary," September 5, 2006, http://www2.ed.gov/policy/elsec/guid/secletter/060905.html.

37. Alyson Klein, "Spellings Is Grilled on NCLB, Reading First," *Education Week* 26, no. 28 (2007): 21, 24.

## *Chapter Six*

# Virtual versus Brick-and-Mortar Public Schools

> In a nutshell: schools are spending billions on technology, even as they cut budgets and lay off teachers, with little proof that this approach is improving basic learning.
>
> —Matt Richtel, *New York Times*

> *Dave*: Hal, I am in command of this ship. I order you to release the manual hibernation control.
>
> *HAL 9000:* I'm sorry, Dave, but in accordance with special subroutine C1435-dash-4, quote, when the crew are dead or incapacitated, the onboard computer must assume control, unquote. I must, therefore, overrule your authority, since you are not in any condition to exercise it intelligently.
>
> —A discussion between HAL 9000 and Dave in *2001: A Space Odyssey*

## DISRUPTION

As noted at the start of this book and throughout, the last thirty years have seen a negative political climate in regard to public schools. Districts have been pressured to cut budgets, resulting in the loss of teachers, librarians, school nurses, and counselors, but money is found, and sometimes squandered, for computers and online instruction. A 2003 national estimate claims US schools spent approximately $80 billion on school computing in the 1990s (Oppenheimer, 2003). In this chapter, the words "online," "virtual," and "personalized learning" are used synonymously.

Technology enhances teaching in positive ways. It can supplement teacher instruction. Also, online education programs, whether they occur in or outside the school, can assist students with disabilities and provide advanced coursework for gifted students. Such programs provide classes that are not available to students who live in rural areas. But should technology replace brick-and-mortar schools—and teachers? Are teacher-led classrooms fast becoming a thing of the past?

In *Disrupting Class: How Disruptive Innovation Will Change the Way the World Learns*, Harvard Business School professor Clayton Christensen claims that not only can computers address individual needs of children, he predicts 50 percent of high school course enrollments will be online by 2019 (Trotter, 2008). This would overhaul public schools as we know them and affect how students learn.

Privatization supporters hail Christensen's book, which takes its place alongside similar books, such as *21st Century Skills and Rethinking How Students Learn* and *Rethinking Education in the Age of Technology: The Digital Revolution and Schooling in America.* Microsoft billionaire and education reformer Bill Gates has called it a "special time in education."[1]

Often called "personalized learning," placing students on the computer with academic programs tailored to their needs sounds enticing. The same individuals who spoke against smaller class sizes to help teachers individualize work for students appear excited about individualizing student learning this way. Online programs might be beneficial to some extent, but what do students miss without a real teacher, and do they learn better this way?

The drive for online assessment, as seen with Common Core State Standards and more specifically the Partnership for Assessment of Readiness for College and Careers and the Smarter Balanced Assessment Consortium, means schools must invest in more computers. But school administrators have been on a computer buying spree for years.

Laptops, Chromebooks, iPads, and other trendy tech devices are high-priority purchases in many school districts. *Education Week*, a popular newspaper for educators, always includes a large listing of ads for numerous tech programs and online learning. But often after a district spends money on technology, the results have been disappointing.

LA Unified School District superintendent John Deasey resigned in 2014, in part due to long-running divisiveness with parents and teachers. He had testified against the teacher's union in *Vergara v. California*. But he also ran into trouble when a $130 million technology record system, called MiSIS, failed to assign students to classes in the beginning of the school year, and he discussed specifics of a new $1.3 billion iPad program, the Common Core Technology Project, with Apple and Pearson before bidding and notifying the public (Bidwell, 2014).

Questions should center on school technology spending and whether it is worth the cost. Plenty of examples demonstrate the failure of technology to make an impact on student test scores. The Kyrene School District in Arizona struggled with budgetary problems, including an inability to provide teachers with raises, yet they invested approximately $33 million into technology. Despite students having access to interactive screens, laptops, and software, school test scores in reading and math were stagnant (Richtel, 2011).

In Tucson, Arizona, the Vail Unified School District spent $850 per laptop for 350 students as opposed to a set of textbooks costing $500 to $600. But students played video games and logged on to illicit websites, and grades and test scores showed little improvement (Hu, 2007). Teachers also needed better preparation on how to incorporate laptops into the classroom setting, and laptops, they found, also cost additional repair fees.

## ONLINE SCHOOLS

A study by the National Education Policy Center (NEPC) found that, by 2011, about forty states operated or authorized full-time or part-time online schools (Glass and Welner, 2011). Online charter schools, many for profit, have little oversight and are costly to taxpayers. Studies to date have looked mostly at online progress in reading and math instruction.

The NEPC study also found that while computer programs may show similar academic gains when compared to face-to-face instruction, this kind of computer usage still involves interpersonal connection to a teacher. While spending tax dollars for expensive full-time virtual programs might be popular, indications are that it does not work *as well* as old-fashioned teaching. When studies show student success with technology, it is often unclear if the improvement is due to computers or outside factors. It could be due to teacher experience or teacher professional development using technology.

The Illinois Online Network listed problems surrounding online learning, summarized below.

- Students do not always have access to good technology.

- Instructors might be lacking preparation.
- Students are not always self-disciplined, well organized, and self-motivated to use technology correctly.
- Problems with the equipment can arise, such as slow connectivity or power outages.
- Online facilitators do not always communicate well with the students.
- Administrators of the online program might worry more about making a profit.
- Online classes might be too large.
- Some subjects do not lend themselves to online instruction.
- Curriculum and instructor qualifications might be questionable. (Illinois Online Network)

Along with and despite a shortage of research covering online schooling, school proponents for online schooling lobby legislators who fund *more* technology. The 2008 report "Keeping Pace with K–12 Online Learning" states, "There are now so many schools, districts, state agencies, and nonprofit organizations offering online courses at the K–12 level that tracking them is nearly impossible, and all states have at least some minor online learning options."[2] This occurs despite knowing that problems *exist* with such programs.

In Colorado, taxpayers spent $100 million in one year alone on online schools, even when those schools failed and students fell behind (Mitchell and Hubbard, 2011). Traditional public schools had their funds diverted to online schools, but when students failed with the online programs, they returned to public school!

Some complain about students and *too much* technology—that is, questionable video games, cyberbullying, and an increased use of TV, texting, and online socializing. Many parents want their children to *scale back* on computer usage in favor of face-to-face communication. A student might be in front of a computer all day. No one can predict the long-term personal and social ramifications of adding to all of this full-time online schooling.

Parents might be deceived into believing technology will provide their children with educational advantages, but overexposure to computers, especially in elementary school, could stifle a child's social development and be risky to their health. New gadgets might be fun to explore, but early childhood demands play and physical activity, not a constant online presence.

This raises the question: How young is too young for online schools? In the 1998 book *Failure to Connect: How Computers Affect Our Children's Minds—and What We Can Do About It*, educational psychologist Jane M. Healy writes extensively about the problems associated with computers and young children. She describes accompanying physical ailments involving too much computer usage (i.e., eye and back strain, carpal tunnel syndrome, and headaches).

Healy states, "An atmosphere of hysteria surrounds the rush to connect even preschoolers to electronic brains. Of the ten best-selling children's CD-ROM titles sold in 1996, four are marketed for children beginning at age three. Computer programs are advertised for children as young as eighteen months."[3] This has not stopped states from jumping onto the online school bandwagon for young and older students.

The Florida Virtual School (FLVS) is one of the earliest and largest online schools in the country. The FLVS began in 1997 offering supplemental classes, assisting students in obtaining alternative high school credits, and providing advanced instruction for gifted students. It started out as Florida's Virtual High School but changed its name when it branched into elementary education.

In 2009, despite state budget problems, Florida *required* school districts to offer full-time online instruction for elementary through high school. Eventually, the legislature required *all students* to take at least one online course. This raised questions as to whether FLVS provided vouchers for homeschooled and students in private school.

Like Florida, in 2006, Michigan required each student to take an online course in order to graduate. Alabama followed with a similar requirement. Michigan relies on the Michigan Virtual School, which claims they use certified teachers, but which, like Florida, contract out to various companies (i.e., Microsoft's CareerForward).

Sometimes, though the worth of online instruction is unproven, it appears to be an either-or proposition. This pits traditional schooling against technology. In 2011, in Miami, students walked into class expecting to meet their teacher and instead were greeted with a facilitator (overseer) and a room full of computers (Herrera, 2011). School districts might save on teacher salaries with such a setup, but they are likely shortchanging students in the long run.

Studies about replacing teachers with online schooling are usually at the university level because college online programs have existed longer. The findings for college online programs indicate that those who administer the programs are not always happy about how they are treated.

Two surveys by the National Association of State Universities and Land-Grant Colleges found professors and administrators of virtual programs also worried about budget cuts (Shieh, 2009). Professors found courses could be burdensome, and they expressed concern about not being rewarded for the time and effort they put into the online programs. Some 70 percent of faculty felt student results were inferior, and many questioned whether students were disciplined enough to participate in online learning. If such concern exists over college online programs, how much worry is there about virtual elementary and high school instruction?

Questions are raised about Massive Open Online Courses (MOOCS), which have become popular with universities such as MIT, Harvard, Stanford, and others. While open access to learning might first appear all-inclusive, it raises serious questions about what constitutes education and the meaning of a degree. Research also found that those who have difficulty in school are less likely to complete MOOCS (Konnikova, 2014).

Online schooling is costly and it is not without problems. Plagiarizing and cheating are difficult to avoid, though most online programs stress integrity and warn against such behavior. Attempts to cheat have been discouraged. The Florida Virtual School relies on communication between teachers and students and whether teachers can tell if students understand the material. They also use a program called Turnitin to help identify plagiarism and whether a student has copied from the Internet (Albers, 2007).

Edison College in Florida has students take exams in the presence of an instructor, and Troy University uses a form of camera technology for monitoring students. The computer is locked while testing takes place, and fingerprints are authenticated. Webcams and a microphone are placed in a reflective, ball-like ornament that records audio and video feedback. Instructors watch and note student movement. Such personal intrusion, however, raises questions about privacy.

In 2015, three independent research institutions conducted a national study of online charter schools. Mathematica Policy Research, the Center on Reinventing Public Education, and the Center for Research on Education Outcomes (CREDO) found concerns relating to online instruction in charter schools.

Troubling findings included the fact that students had to pace themselves on the computer, and they received much less teacher contact time than those in traditional schools. Online schools expected parents to fill in the learning gaps found when students relied on computers and not teachers. Open admission failed to screen good student candidates for online instruction, and accountability provisions were lacking. And CREDO's report found that online charter schools had much weaker academic growth in reading and math compared to traditional public schools.

## PRIVATIZING ONLINE SCHOOLS

While virtual schools run by the state are controversial, they are, in most cases, run with oversight by credentialed teachers. This is different from for-profit online schools. The biggest problem with online schooling is the glut of unregulated schools flooding a virtual school marketplace.

The Florida Virtual School ran into trouble in 2013 when a bill was passed by the state legislature to open the door to outside online school vendors (for example, K12 Inc., Kaplan, and VSchoolz). This meant cuts to the FLVS and loss of staff (McGrory, 2013). Despite the past success of the FLVS, and without proof other virtual school programs would do better, the state legislature favored an influx of outside for-profit virtual programs—leaning away from FLVS toward choice and the marketplace.

FLVS always had its own attachment to the for-profit industry. Despite being partly state regulated, it mixed with Connections Academy. Connections is a private online company started by Sylvan Ventures, and owned by Pearson, to provide elementary online instruction. Connections once had ties to the controversial American Legislative Exchange Council (ALEC) described in chapter 1. Like ALEC, Connections has always supported privatizing public schools, and according to SourceWatch, they pushed "a national agenda to replace brick and mortar classrooms with computers and replace actual teachers with 'virtual' teachers."[4]

Connections quit their association with ALEC during the trial surrounding the controversial ALEC-backed "Stand Your Ground" law and the shooting death of a teenager in Florida. But SourceWatch also wrote a complex report surrounding the far-reaching influence of Connections Academy, including how they support other virtual for-profit companies and have given money to Jeb Bush's Foundation for Excellence in Education.[5]

Governor Bush has been an advocate of virtual charter schools. He has toured the country to promote technology, gave a commencement speech for the Ohio online school Electronic Classroom of Tomorrow, and helped start

Digital Learning Now, a group to promote public funding for virtual classrooms (Mencimer, 2011).

Connections Academy along with K12 Inc. backed the Virtual Public Schools Act, which gives virtual schools the same rights as brick-and-mortar schools, only without the overhead costs of school furniture, playgrounds, in-person teachers, school bands, and more. Regardless of the questionable academic records for both these virtual schools, they make huge profits from tax dollars.

## K12 INC.

> At K12, we are committed to creating shareholder value.
>
> —K12 Inc.[6]

While chairman of the Federal Communications Commission, Reed Hundt asked former Republican education secretary William Bennett (Reagan) to help obtain legislation to pay for Internet access for America's schools and libraries. Hundt said Bennett told him, "He would not help, because he did not want public schools to obtain new funding, new capability, new tools for success. He wanted them, he said, to fail so that they could be replaced with vouchers, charter schools, religious schools, and other forms of private education."[7]

But with support from senators Olympia Snowe (R-ME) and Jay Rockefeller (D-WV), President Clinton and Vice President Al Gore put the provision in the Telecommunications Law of 1996. Despite Bennett's opposition, the Internet became almost as much a reality for poor children as those in wealthier schools.[8]

Bennett never liked public schools, and he originally denounced computers. But with $10 million invested by financier and junk bond dealer Michael Milken, who spent prison time for security fraud, Bennett jumped on the online bandwagon (Walsh, 2001). Support for the computer program came from Milken, creator of the Knowledge Universe Learning Group; David Gelernter, Yale professor of computer science; Ron Packard, from Milken's program; and Lowell Milken, Michael Milken's brother. Chester Finn Jr., always outspoken against public schools, also assisted. Finn ended his involvement with the venture in 2007.

K12 Inc. started as a program for children whose parents wanted to home-school for religious reasons. But it expanded, receiving lucrative contracts from state and local school districts for charter and traditional public school use. While public schools were being shut down due to test scores and teachers and curriculums were scrutinized like never before, few taxpayers questioned the funding and lacking oversight of K12 Inc.

The title "K12" is the base name, and the schools started out using the state name and "Virtual Academy" (i.e., Florida Virtual Academy, Arizona Virtual Academy, etc.). The titles were easily confused with state virtual schools (i.e., Florida Virtual School, Arizona Virtual School, etc.). The Florida Virtual School filed a lawsuit against K12 for trademark infringement, and, in 2014, the Florida Supreme Court ruled that the Florida Virtual School had the authority to pursue the case (Turner, 2014).

It is not easy to avoid the ads for K12. They are on the radio, pop up on computer screens, and are on television. As more parents became dissatisfied with fewer public school services due to budget cuts, K12 might seem like a legitimate substitute to schooling. But while the program has been advertised as successful, the facts show the opposite.

In 2004, educator/writer Susan Ohanian wondered why few look at K12's virtual material content. She pretended to be children and put herself through the program. What she discovered was a heavy emphasis on war, with warlike coloring pages, and the primary program "introduces the occult, superstition, and magic" and "sex and gore."[9] K12 was "relentless in its presentation of map skills, warriors, and the hierarchy of the Catholic Church," and it "rarely provides a moral message about some of the appalling historical events it includes."[10] Ohanian could find nothing personalized about the program.

Concerns about K12 also surfaced in Arkansas. The Department of Education awarded grants for the program despite K12 scoring lower on a series of independent reviews and one other unfunded program (*eSchool News*, 2004). Grants totaling $4 million from the US Department of Education (ED) went to K12. A charter school setup included K12, and 60 percent of the program funding went to homeschooled students. Some 15 percent went to private schools—or the student's school was unknown.

In Arizona, concerns were raised about student achievement and the easy way students could cheat using K12 (Ryman and Kossan, 2011). Parental time and commitment are a necessity with the program. According to the K12 website, parents must be willing to teach their own children and spend at least three to five hours a day administering the program. Children work by themselves the rest of the time. Parental demands decrease as the child gets older, when they can work independently.

But K12 is funded by states despite doubts about the program. As far back as 2003, questions rose as to why Florida Department of Education officials allowed kindergartners and first-graders to enroll in virtual for-profit schools run through Bennett's program and a smaller virtual program run by Sylvan. The move, according to a *Palm Beach Post* analysis, cost taxpayers $950,000 (Miller and Date, 2003). A $4,800 student voucher to the Florida Virtual Academy included loaning a computer and modem for Internet access.

In 2008, retired English teacher, David A. Safier, presented a critical review on Blog for Arizona, when it was learned that K12's Arizona Virtual Academy sent English essays to India for grading. While such practice raises many quality concerns, the main outrage involved the lack of privacy protections for students. America's Family Educational Rights and Privacy Act means American school teachers must be fingerprinted and receive background checks. In this case, K12's Arizona Virtual Academy contracted with Socratic Learning, Inc., and grading was done through Tutors Worldwide based in India.

It is not clear how much outsourcing still occurs with online programs in general. *Education Week* reported in 2008 that K12 had ended outsourcing (Trotter, 2008). Comments to the article revealed angry parents who felt betrayed after being led to believe that real teachers from America were helping their children. In San Mateo, California, the virtual academy's budget included $642,304 in management fees for nine hundred students in their homes and $2.7 million for materials and technology (Pogash, 2010). Each student participating in K12 received $5,105 in state and federal money—$375 more than children in regular public school there.

In 2011, it was learned that almost 60 percent of K12 students in the Agora Cyber Charter School (K12) were behind in math, and 50 percent lagged behind traditional public schools in reading. One-third of K12 students failed to graduate, and students quit not long after starting the program. Despite questions about the use of tax dollars to fund K12's poor performance, many tied to Wall Street boasted of the school's success (Saul, 2011).

Other states such as Florida and Colorado looked into allegations that uncertified teachers were used in the program, student-teacher ratios were high with possibly 275 students per teacher, student grading was easy, and the program accepted funding for known high-risk students who would likely drop out (Hood, 2011).

Students receive funding diverted from traditional public schools to purchase the program. If they decide they do not like it and want to return to public school, K12 keeps the money. While politicians push traditional public school students to spend more time in school, K12 students bragged about having to go to school only three hours a day (Layton and Brown, 2011).

In 2012, the Georgia Department of Education threatened to close a K12 online charter school, Georgia Cyber Academy, because it did not provide the necessary services for students with disabilities (O'Connor, 2012). K12 lacked evidence of success overall, but many students stayed home to work on the program. The company should have also been increasing the salaries of teachers for these students, but they spent less than charter schools and school districts when it came to special education instruction (Miron and Urschel, 2012).

In 2012, Tennessee state senator Andy Berke (D) raised concerns about the dismal outcomes of K12 in Union County. The school district funded the virtual academy, enrolling 1,800 students. Berke questioned state law allowing the program to continue with "bottom of the bottom" results.[11] K12 cost $5.04 million in the 2011 to 2012 school year—funding that could have gone to public schools. The cost was also expected to rise to $8.23 million for the new school year. K12 is still funded in Tennessee.

The US Department of Education and state education departments have funded K12 despite questions as to whether it is religiously biased. In a 2001 Belief.net online interview, Bennett said, "Our curriculum has a point of view. We believe in certain things, we believe in certain ideas of right and wrong, and of knowledge and truth and that's manifest in our program. We're centered in the Judeo-Christian tradition, we do not ignore faith and religion, we do not ignore the arguments against evolution, because there are some."[12]

When asked about diversity, homosexuality, and people of color, Bennett added:

> We don't take much cognizance of that. We address children as children. I think of them more as children of God, as moral and spiritual beings, and Americans. Those are the labels that I'm interested in. I'm not much interested in their color, or other accidents. And I think that the more we do of the approach we're taking, the better.[13]

Even after Bennett's resignation as an employee and as chairman and member of the K12's Board of Directors, his influence is still felt. K12 became one of the largest operators of virtual schools across the country, despite it never proving itself a worthy program. In 2013, another for-profit education company managed by K12 accused them of using "dubious and sometimes fraudulent tactics to mask astronomical rates of student turnover" in virtual schools.[14]

School officials still complain that K12 siphons money from public schools. Court challenges by parents and the teachers unions in Minnesota and Wisconsin alleged that K12 made contractual agreements for three to ten years and operates in about twenty-five states and abroad. Pennsylvania was also involved in litigation concerning online instruction, questioning the justification of using state funds to buy for-profit virtual programs for home-schooled children and students in charter schools. But cases like this have been derailed or dropped, and programs like K12 continue to thrive.

That K12 flourishes must put smiles on the faces of school reformers who always wanted privatization through technology. But the fact that it repeatedly fails while drawing tax dollars does not bode well for free market ideology. Bennett, and other Milton Friedman followers, are demonstrating well with K12 vouchers and charter schools that free market choice fails. Unfortunately, these unsuccessful programs will continue to plague America's schoolchildren long after they are shown to be insufficient.

William Bennett is the best-selling author of *The Book of Virtues*, *The Children's Book of Virtues*, and other books promoting moral beliefs. This is the same William Bennett who in 2003 admitted to gambling away millions and who had to apologize for suggesting that an effective way to reduce crime is to abort black babies.

He did a stint as a CNN commentator and is currently host of a nationally syndicated radio program, *Morning in America*. He is not out of the education business. As senior advisor to Project Lead the Way, a nonprofit that focuses on hands-on engineering projects for public, private, and charter schools, he still advocates school privatization. High-level administrators from corporations such as Dow Chemical and Lockheed Martin usually sit on the Board of Directors of Project Lead the Way.

In the meantime, the National Education Policy Center reported that K12 students were falling further behind in math and reading than students in brick-and-mortar schools (Mathis and Miron, 2012). The suggestion was made to make funding to virtual schools contingent upon student completion. In 2015, K12 Inc. reported $948.3 million in revenues.[15]

## SCHOOL OF THE FUTURE

One big advocate for online instruction is Bill Gates. In 2006, the Philadelphia School of the Future, considered a public school, opened in Philadelphia. The school's price tag in tax dollars was $63 million. Microsoft provided consultants to model their business principles. Interactive learning centers replaced the library. Students used laptops for everything with assistance from multimedia specialists.

The 170 members of the student body expressed excitement, as did the school district, which heavily promoted the school. *Philadelphia Magazine* credited school district CEO Paul Vallas for approaching Gates with the idea for the school, and they named it the Philadelphia School of the Future (SOF). Vallas later became the superintendent of the mostly charter school Recovery School district in New Orleans.

The following is a description of the SOF—promoted as a Leadership in Energy and Environmental Design (LEED) School, written about in *Philadelphia Magazine*:

> They'll [students] pass through a hidden weapons-detection system and step into a wide corridor dubbed "Main Street." They'll swipe their "smart cards," and a screen will display their photographs and register their attendance. They'll move quickly, carrying only a small laptop from class to class and home at night (no more overloaded backpacks). Passing the administrative offices and the "interactive learning center" (read: a library without books), they'll come to a mall-style food court, where purchases will be tracked with the same card. (No more telling Mom you had broccoli while really subsisting on Kit Kats and Snapple.)
>
> In the gym, plasma-screen televisions and video cameras will bring pro-style instant-replay access to the varsity level, and outside, a futuristic anti-graffiti coating on the walls will make washing off tags easier. This technological utopia of high-density fiber-optic cable will be virtually paperless, although there will be printers on hand (just in case). And the entire building—a green building, complete with solar panels and grassy roof—is wired, powered and online.[16]

While the school opened with much fanfare, in 2009, an American Enterprise Institute (AEI) panel determined the "Microsoft inspired project, a 'lesson in failure.'"[17] The school had a high turnover of leaders and staff despite the Microsoft training and emphasis on twenty-first-century skills. Amid the state-of-the-art school facility and the emphasis on technology, many questioned why Microsoft trainers failed to communicate their vision for the school (i.e., "6 'I's: introspection, investigation, inclusion, innovation, implementation, and—again—introspection"). No one seemed to understand how to apply the vision to real life.

In the AEI description, Drexel University's Jan Biros, associate vice president for instructional technology support and a former member of the SOF Curriculum Planning Committee, stated, "We naively thought, I guess, that by providing a beautiful building and great resources, these things would automatically yield change. They didn't."[18] Ideas seemed not to translate into practical practices for the school. With rapid staff turnover, including three superintendents and four principals, Microsoft's vision appeared lost in translation.

In 2009, several weeks after the AEI report, Bill Gates spoke at the National Conference of State Legislatures' annual legislative summit about his education ideas. He encouraged lawmakers to use federal stimulus money "to spark educational innovation, spread best practices and improve accountability," and he noted that teachers should be "rewarded for effectiveness and not just for seniority and master's degrees."[19] He made no mention of the Philadelphia School of the Future.

In 2010, supporters learned that many graduating seniors were disappointed in the school (Russ, 2010). SAT results lagged. Students realized they lacked a solid foundation in the core subjects, perhaps due partially to the lack of textbooks. They also complained of a lack of experienced educators.

Still, *USA Today* lavished praise on the school, claiming students were graduating and going to college—except for those who went to summer school (Matheson, 2010). Little was said about any of the school's later test scores. The report "Microsoft 'School of the Future' in Philly Finally in a Groove?" ends with a question mark. What's happening with the school now? That's a good question. The Microsoft School of the Future looked like the prototype of the kind of school corporations hoped to convert most schools into in the future, even with its less-than-stellar results.

## ROCKETSHIP

Created in 2007 by two entrepreneurs who claimed the schools would help struggling students, Rocketship was promoted as a successful alternative for struggling students. Here again, some would like the for-profit online schools to be the prototype for future schooling. Past members of the board of directors include Sheryl Sandberg, COO of Facebook; Reed Hastings, CEO of Netflix; Jonathan Chadwick, CFO of Skype; and Bill Gurley, Benchmark Capital general partner. Hedge funds, venture capitalists, and investment banks support the schools (Lafer, 2013).

Despite persistent declarations about increased achievement, Rocketship is not as successful as those who support them claim. Math and reading are the only real subjects taught—called blended learning. But teachers who work there look to be inexperienced, and they focus on high-stakes testing and data collection.

In Wisconsin, where antiunion attempts to dismantle public schools have been fierce, Rocketship is attempting to take over more traditional public schools. The Republican Party has supported Rocketship, but the school has had problems. Katy Venskus, vice president of policy for Rocketship and former chief of staff to ex-Wisconsin state senator Jeff Plate, was convicted of felony theft in 2002 from an abortion rights group and for stealing from her former lobbying firm, but she was still allowed to lobby in Wisconsin for Rocketship (Stein, 2010).

In 2014, tennis star Andre Agassi showed up in Nashville to tour a new Rocketship charter school. He and businessman Bobby Turner helped bankroll the facility, along with costs for thirty-nine other new charter schools in twelve cities within two years. Metro Nashville School Board member Amy Frogge said, "Schools should be the very embodiment of community, but some folks want to turn schools into a marketplace. This can pervert educational outcomes for students, particularly our most vulnerable children."[20]

Agassi responded, "From my background as a capitalist—I know that may be offensive—I recognize that the only way to truly cure a problem in society is to create a sustainable solution, harnessing market forces to make money. The reality is, there's no secret: Making money and making societal change need not be exclusive."[21]

Rocketship charter schools employ noncredentialed college graduates to monitor students who work online. Currently eleven Rocketships dot the landscape in the Bay Area, and one is in Milwaukee and three in Nashville. Another school will open in Washington, DC, in 2016.

Rocketship charter schools were rapidly expanding across the country, but poor test scores and pushback by parents, teachers, and citizens has slowed construction of more schools. San Jose parents, led by Brett Bymaster, filed a lawsuit against the chain charter (Noguchi, 2014). The group expressed concern over the secrecy of Rocketship and the lack of community involvement in the school.

Stop Rocketship Education Now! is a website about problems surrounding the charter school. Many of the school's students are Hispanic, and the argument is that Hispanic communities should not resort to outside organizations and individuals taking over their public schools.

In 2014, rural Morgan Hill, California, near Silicon Valley, also rejected a Rocketship application. Another charter school faced pressure, after parents, teachers, and the teachers union put up resistance (Bacon, 2014). Parents and groups such as Stop Rocketship Now! are successfully slowing down future Rocketships.

Questions have also been raised about Khan Academy, a tutorial program heavily promoted by Bill Gates, and Ampify, another online program. Joel Klein, once chancellor of New York City Schools, and Chris Cerf, former New Jersey Education Commissioner, also president and COO of Edison Schools, have been involved with Amplify.

The curriculum, assessment, data-driven program, and an independent subsidiary of News Corporation, is owned by Australian media mogul Rupert Murdock. That so many school reformers who support public school privatization are involved with technology and online programs raises concern.

## STUDENT PRIVACY

Technology has changed the way a student's information is stored, but the laws surrounding who has access to this material, and what will be done with it, is troubling to parents. The Family Educational Rights and Privacy Act (FERPA) is a federal law that once protected the privacy of student education records in schools receiving funds from the US Department of Education. It was commonplace to have parents share their student's records with transferring schools, financial aid groups, health and safety organizations, or school officials. Parents provided written permission.

But changes to the law were made in 2008 and 2011. FERPA usually requires parental consent, but allowance was made for record disclosure, minus consent, to questionable parties under less restrictive conditions. Schools can provide outside organizations a student's name, address and phone number, date and place of birth, honors and awards, and attendance dates. Schools must inform parents about directory information, and parents can request that their child's information not be disclosed.

Who gets to see the information, and why do they want it? In this age of high-stakes testing, data has become king. Giving your student's information to outside companies allows them to target your student for resources that, they claim, will address student learning needs. It's seen as one way to collect and disseminate information to promote seamless learning.

At the center of the controversy with Common Core State Standards (CCSS) was inBloom, a $100 million database that promised to help teachers tailor learning to skill levels, provide parents better information about the learning process, save teachers and schools time and money, and enhance data privacy and security safely. But inBloom worried parents who feared personal student information would be released to companies who would profit at their child's expense. Parents disliked both CCSS and sharing information about their children.

Bill Gates invested heavily in inBloom and spoke in its favor. But parent activists such as Leonie Haimson in New York and others sought to educate the public about the perils that exist when others have access to student information. Concerns surrounding data collection and data mining continued to grow.

In 2014, inBloom announced it was shutting down largely in response to the tough pushback of the New York State United Teachers and parents who did not want their student's information violated. This was seen as a victory for parents, but Haimson warned to watch out for alternative forms of inBloom (2014). Some states are enacting privacy laws to curb parental concerns.

## COMPETENCY-BASED EDUCATION

Competency-Based Education (CBE) is not new. Teachers pretest students to find out what they know. They provide instruction that addresses what students need to learn. Finally, they reassess to see if the instruction made a difference. If the teaching worked, the teacher moves on. If the student has not learned the information, the teacher rethinks his or her teaching strategy and does something different to teach the skill. Special education teachers have always known about CBE because it is used with Individual Educational Plans.

Computers are useful to present basic skills through a CBE approach. PLATO, for example, is a computer-based education system that permits students to work independently on skill review in reading, writing, math, science, and life and career skills. The program provides pretesting and post-testing, and students move on only when they master a skill.

There is nothing wrong with programs like PLATO or CBE per se. Teachers have relied on technology to complement their teaching. But this kind of instruction is being promoted today as a be-all program. Those who see online instruction as all-encompassing think sticking students on the computer to get all their instruction online is the way to go. The push to replace brick-and-mortar schools with virtual instruction is a reality through Competency-Based Education (CBE). Yet the idea that CBE is all that it takes to lead a student to college and career is misguided.

CBE is synonymous with Proficiency-Based Education, Performance-Based Education, and Standards-Based Education. These titles, under the umbrella of CBE, are promoted as "personalized learning." But this is much different from what most people think of when they hear those words. The title, "personalized learning," implies students will get special attention from their teachers. One envisions a small class size where teachers get to know students—where they can teach academic and social skills. But that is not what personalized learning involves.

While teachers have long argued in favor of smaller class sizes, and research is well documented that class size reduction can be advantageous for students, school reformers have long been critical of lowering class sizes. Bill Gates spoke out against it, suggesting teachers receive incentives for *larger* class sizes (deVise, 2011).

CBE-style personalized learning occurs through technology. Class size does not matter since students work online to learn skills. Pictures advertise huge numbers of students sitting side by side in carrels working online.

Along with Competency-Based Learning, blended learning and flipping the classroom are used to diminish the role of the teacher and place added emphasis on technology. Blended learning involves students being in charge of their time, place, and pace of learning school material. Flipping the classroom means students do the bulk of their work online at home. They listen to lectures on the computer and use the classroom the next day to ask questions.

Tom Vander Ark, who once worked with the Gates Foundation, is a proponent of CBE. And some of the same people from the Gates Foundation, who worked on standards years ago, have been involved with CBE. The Carnegie Corporation of New York, Nellie Mae Education Foundation, and others support Competency Works from the International Association for

K–12 Online Learning (iNACOL), which is all about CBE (Worthen and Pace, 2014).

CBE is the ultimate end of teacher-led instruction in public schools. Its promotion of personalized learning only means that students must master a skill at their level before moving forward. While the skills are individualized, they are the same skills other students are required to achieve. Because every skill is measured before moving forward to the next skill, testing is ongoing and embedded in the lesson.

CBE is also connected to Common Core State Standards, which are controversial and unproven. Like Common Core, online instruction has no proven track record, and CBE is rote learning at best. It does not look as if CBE will end any time soon. At the time of this writing, teachers are expressing concern about the takeover of this form of instruction at the expense of more creative teaching.

## CONCLUSION: REAL SCHOOLS AND TEACHERS

Technology might complement schooling, but it can also be used recklessly at a high cost both economically and academically to students and taxpayers. Little evidence exists that online schooling costs less or is better at teaching. It is not known what the long-term effects a top-heavy technology curriculum will be on students.

Competency-Based Education seems like little more than paperless drilling of basic skills. No proof shows that embedding the skills a child is expected to learn into technology and online assessment will be better than teacher instruction. Grave questions surround the loss of social interaction. How will online instruction affect a child's ability to connect with others?

Instead of school districts imposing technology on students with little forethought, often resulting in the squandering of funds, here is a checklist of what school administrators should consider when purchasing new technology:

- Don't expect technology to create miracles—be realistic.
- Is this the best use of school funding?
- Be careful about copying a successful program elsewhere. What works in one school district might fail in another.
- Take time to plan ahead. What is needed overall to support technology?

- Ensure that teachers will get the necessary preparation to use the technology.
- Know how to evaluate programs that go along with the technology.
- Do not gamble on technology if unsure about how it will be used.
- Carefully calculate the overall long-term costs.
- Consider equity issues involving multicultural and special education. (Trucano, 2010)

Before school districts invest further in online charter schools and programs to take the place of public schooling, education researchers William Mathis and Gary Miron recommend a moratorium on the creation of virtual schools. They suggest that such schools should be transparent and demonstrate better accountability—and that the funding formula be revised for better financial oversight (2012). Consideration of any online program should involve questions about student/teacher ratio, teacher credentials, and/or authenticity of student work with online programming. How are students monitored so cheating does not occur?

Parents who choose homeschooling should also be wary of any online program making promises that cannot be delivered. They should research beyond the ads, or what their school district tells them about technology. Any online program demanding a purchase upfront with no promise of a refund should be avoided. Until safeguards are put in place, parents should tread carefully when it comes to online instruction, and they should focus more on supporting rich and varied content provided by credentialed teachers in traditional public schools.

The most concerning information to give technology enthusiasts pause comes from the Organization for Economic Cooperation and Development, which looked at fifteen-year-olds and their computer use in thirty-one nations and regions. They found that reading and math scores on the Program for International Student Assessment (PISA) were lower for students who used computers more rather than those who used technology less at school (OECD, 2015).

The report reminds readers that adults are in charge of creating a technology safe and academically useful environment for students. School districts should reassess both the cost and usage of technology in the classroom. It does not suggest that online instruction is at all close to replacing teachers and brick-and-mortar public schools.

Personalizing education for students is a worthy goal in America's public schools, but technology is only part of what that means for students. Technology can be a beneficial tool for teachers to supplement lessons, but replacing teacher expertise and schools with online instruction is irresponsible. Focusing only on skill mastery, a cold, calculated form of instruction, shortchanges students. In the long run, it could prove devastating to students, public schools, and America's future.

## NOTES

1. "Catching on at Last," *The Economist*, June 29, 2013.
2. John Watson, Butch Gemin, and Jennifer Ryan, "Keeping Pace with K–12 Online Learning: A Review of State-Level Policy and Practice," November 2008, http://www.kpk12.com/wp-content/uploads/KeepingPace_2008.pdf.
3. Jane M. Healy, *Failure to Connect: How Computers Affect Our Children's Minds—and What We Can Do About It* (New York: Touchstone, 1998), 20.
4. Sourcewatch: The Center for Media and Democracy, "Connections Academy," http://www.sourcewatch.org/index.php/Connections_Academy.
5. Ibid.
6. K12 Transforming Education, Transforming Lives, 2010 Annual Report.
7. Reed Hundt, The Coffee House Politics, 2005, http://www.susanohanian.org/outrage_fetch.php?id=351.
8. Ibid.
9. Susan Ohanian, "The K12 Virtual Primary School History Curriculum: A Participant's-Eye View," Arizona State University, Education Policy Research Unit (EPRU), January 1, 2004, http://nepc.colorado.edu/publication/the-k12-virtual-primary-school-history-curriculum-a-participants-eye-view.
10. Ibid.
11. Zack MacMillan, "Chattanooga Senator Slaps Virtual School Company for 'Results at Bottom of the Bottom,'" Politifact Tennessee, October 7, 2012, http://www.politifact.com/tennessee/statements/2012/oct/07/andy-berke/chattanooga-senator-slaps-virtual-school-company-r/.
12. Wendy Schuman, "Bill Bennett's Online Schoolhouse," 2001, http://www.beliefnet.com/Love-Family/Parenting/2001/10/Bill-Bennetts-Online-Schoolhouse.aspx?p=3.
13. Ibid.
14. Benjamin Herold, "K12 Inc. Sued over For-Profit Education Company's Tax-Subsidized Funding Manipulation," *Huffington Post*, January 23, 2013, http://www.huffingtonpost.com/2013/01/23/k12-inc-sued-over-for-pro_n_2535359.html.
15. K12 News Release, http://investors.k12.com/phoenix.zhtml?c=214389&p=irol-newsArticle&ID=2075296#.Vm5lpr-n-wY.
16. Christine Smallwood, "Top Schools: Is This Really the School of the Future?" *Philadelphia Magazine*, September 7, 2006.
17. Meris Stansbury, "School of the Future: Lessons in Failure," *eSchool News*, June 1, 2009, http://www.eschoolnews.com/2009/06/01/school-of-the-future-lessons-in-failure/.
18. Ibid.

19. Kathy Matheson, "Bill Gates: Better Data Mean Better Schools," *Associated Press*, July 21, 2009.

20. Joey Garrison, "Andre Agassi, in Nashville, Embraces Investor-Led Approach to Help Schools," *Tennessean*, September 17, 2014.

21. Ibid.

# Conclusion

> Public schools provide public forums for discussing the critical issues of how we prepare our children for the future. Many of the experiments now under way remove parents from that discussion and reconvene in corporate boardrooms. This is not a good path for a democracy to take. Among the freedoms that the attacks of September 11 reminded us is how open a society we have and how precious that openness is. It would be tragic to lose that openness in the realm of education.
>
> —Gerald W. Bracey[1]

Public schools are for all children. They should reject no one. *A Nation at Risk* sent an alarming message that public schools were failing, even endangering the country. This overexaggerated message, along with lackluster solutions, never led to improved schools. Instead, the school reforms that were put in place led to the corporatization of public schools.

Now we see unregulated charter schools and vouchers. Students receive false messages about job preparation and the global economy, and religious interference leads to a change in the way schools treat students. The deprofessionalization of the role of educators means those with little understanding of children and how they learn are the new school leaders. And the bold overemphasis on technology raises questions about the future of schooling.

But parents and educators are fighting back to reclaim public schools. Community and state organizations across the country are standing up to those who want to privatize every facet of education. While America's public schools will always reflect society and the problems found there, they should also provide a beacon of hope for students and families.

Americans want better public schools for all children. They understand that an educated populace serves everyone. Both parents and teachers are uniting and speaking out against the school changes that have led them to feel disenfranchised.

It is difficult to fight influence and funding from the Gates Foundation and other corporations. It might appear hopeless. But Americans are pushing back on misguided school reform like never before. Through the grassroots groups mentioned here and social media, many are fighting to save their public schools. Perhaps those who seek to privatize public schools will one day see that public schools were never as bad as they thought, and that the heart of a good democracy rests in the public school system. I believe we will not fail, and our public schools will someday be stronger and better than ever before.

## NOTE

1. Gerald W. Bracey, *What You Should Know About the War Against America's Public Schools* (Boston, MA: Allyn & Bacon, 2003), 177.

# References


*Abington School District v. Schempp*, 374 US 203 (1963).

Achieve. http://www.achieve.org/contributors.

Ahearn, Eileen. "Public Charter Schools and Students with Disabilities." ERIC Digest. E609. 2001. http://www.ericdigests.org/2002-2/public.htm.

Albers, Katherine. "Poll: Tougher Catching Cheating with Online Test Takers, Educators Say." *Naples Daily News*, July 16, 2007.

Álvarez, Brenda. "Eskelsen García: We Are Fearless and We Will Not Be Silent." *NEA Today*, July 6, 2014.

American Federation of Teachers. Foundation Funds. http://www.aft.org/education/well-prepared-and-supported-school-staff/school-improvement/foundation-funds.

American Legislative Exchange Council (ALEC). Education. https://www.alec.org/issue/education/.

"A Nation Prepared: Teachers for the 21st Century: The Report of the Task Force on Teaching as a Profession." Carnegie Forum on Education and the Economy, May 1986. Washington, DC.

Ansary, Tamim. "Education at Risk: Fallout from a Flawed Report." Edutopia. March 9, 2007. http://www.edutopia.org/landmark-education-report-nation-risk.

Anti-Defamation League. "School Vouchers: The Wrong Choice for Public Education." Civil Rights Division. 2012. www.adl.org/religious_freedom/resource_kit/school_vouchers.asp.

Arizona State University. Mary Lou Fulton Teachers College. Secondary Education. http://education.asu.edu/programs/view/bachelor-of-arts-in-education-for-secondary-education.

Ash, Katie. "Vouchers Prove Wild Card for Local Finances." *Education Week* 33, no. 16 (2014): 20, 2.

"The Aspen Declaration." Foundation Documents and Ideas. Josephson Institute of Ethics. 2002.

Axelson, Barb. "Don't Call It Shop." *Technology & Learning* 30, no. 2 (2009): 30–35.

Bacon, David. "Rocketship to Profits." *Rethinking Schools* 29, no. 1 (2014): 24–27.

Baines, Lawrence A. "Deconstructing Teacher Education." *Phi Delta Kappan* 88, no. 4 (2006): 326–28.

Baker, Al. "Culture Warrior, Gaining Ground." *New York Times*, September 27, 2013.

Beilke, Dustin. "Corporate Education Reformers Plot Next Steps at Secretive Meeting." Common Dreams, February 2, 2012. http://www.commondreams.org/view/2012/02/02-9.

Benderly, Beryl Lieff. "Does the US Produce Too Many Scientists?" *Scientific American*, February 22, 2010. http://www.scientificamerican.com/article.cfm?id=does-the-us-produce-too-m.

Benderly, Beryl Lieff. "What Scientist Shortage? The Johnny-Can't-Do-Science Myth Damages US Research." *Columbia Journalism Review* (January/February 2012).

Berliner, David C., and Gene V. Glass. *50 Myths and Lies That Threaten America's Public Schools: The Real Crisis in Education*. New York: Teachers College Press, 2014, 12–17, 209.

Bidwell, Allie. "Los Angeles Schools Chief Steps Down During Investigation." *U.S. News and World Report*. October 16, 2014.

Bifulco, Robert, and Helen F. Ladd. *The Impacts of Charter Schools on Student Achievement: Evidence from North Carolina*. Duke. Working Paper Series SAN04-02. August 2004.

Bill & Melinda Gates Foundation. Measures of Effective Teaching (MET). 2013. http://www.metproject.org/index.php.

Bloom, Molly. "Ohio Edu-Budget 2013: Low-Income Students Everywhere in Ohio Now Eligible for Private School Vouchers." Ohio Eye on Education. State Impact. NPR. http://dev.stateimpact.org/ohio/2013/07/09/h-59-ohio-edu-budget-2013-students-across-ohio-now-eligible-for-private-school-vouchers/.

Blume, Howard. "Backers Want Half of LAUSD Students in Charter Schools in Eight Years, Report Says." *Los Angeles Times*, September 21, 2015.

———. "Charter Schools' Growth Promoting Segregation, Studies Say." *Los Angeles Times*, February 4, 2010.

———. "Key L.A. Unified Staff Positions Are Funded Privately." *Los Angeles Times*, December 16, 2009.

Bridges4Kids. "Court Cases of Interest."www.bridges4kids.org/RecentCourtCases.html.

Broad Academy. http://www.broadcenter.org/academy/.

Broad Institute for School Boards. http://broadeducation.org/about/broad_institute.html.

Broad Prize for Urban Education. http://www.broadprize.org/index.html.

Budde, Ray. "The Evolution of the Charter Concept." *Phi Delta Kappan* 78, no. 1 (1996): 5–6.

Bushaw, William J., and Shane J. Lopez. "Which Way Do We Go? The 45th Annual PDK/Gallup Poll of the Public's Attitudes toward the Public Schools." *Phi Delta Kappan* 93, no. 1 (2013): 10.

Cannon, Kelly. "Locker Room Prayers Common in Utah Public Schools." *Herald Journal*, April 7, 2013.

Caputo, Marc. "Edison Schools Accept Buyout." *Miami Herald*, November 13, 2003.

Carl D. Perkins Career and Technical Education Act of 2006 (Public Law 109-270). http://www2.ed.gov/policy/sectech/leg/perkins/index.html.

Carnegie Corporation of New York. "A Nation Prepared: Teachers for the 21st Century. The Report of the Task Force on Teaching as a Profession." May 1986.

"Catching On at Last." *The Economist*, June 29, 2013. http://www.economist.com/news/briefing/21580136-new-technology-poised-disrupt-americas-schools-and-then-worlds-catching-last.

Cavener, Levi. "Teach for America Falls Short in Special Education." IdahoedNews.org, December 23, 2013.

Ceasar, Stephen. "Officials Address Restroom Problem at Locke High." *Los Angeles Times*, May 13, 2013.

Office of Postsecondary Access, Supper and Success. "Collegiate Development." Carl D. Perkins Career and Technical Education Improvement Act Programs (CTEA), www.highered.nysed.gov/kiap/colldev/VTEA/.

Center for Popular Democracy and the Alliance to Reclaim Our Schools. "The Tip of the Iceberg: Charter School Vulnerabilities to Waste, Fraud, and Abuse," April 2015.

Change the Equation. Featured Programs.http://changetheequation.org/featured-programs/uteach.

Charter School Performance. CREDO. Stanford Education. April 2011. http://credo.stanford.edu/reports/PA%20State%20Report_20110404_FINAL.pdf.

Charter School Scandals. http://charterschoolscandals.blogspot.com/.

Charter Schools USA. Our Schools. http://www.charterschoolsusa.com/schools/.

Chew, Kristina. "Bill Gates Gives ALEC Big $$$ to 'Reform Education.'" Care 2 Make a Difference. December 5, 2011. http://www.care2.com/causes/bill-gates-gives-alec-big-to-reform-education.html?page=1.

Children's Scholarship Fund Charlotte. National Board of Advisors. http://csfcharlotte.org/about/csf-national/.

"Church, Choice, and Charters: A New Wrinkle for Public Education?" *Harvard Law Review* 122, no. 6 (2009): 1750.

Clawson, Laura. "Gates Foundation Works to Influence Education Laws through Big Grant to ALEC." *Daily Kos*, December 6, 2011. http://www.dailykos.com/story/2011/12/06/1042841/-Gates-Foundation-works-to-influence-education-laws-through-big-grant-to-ALEC.

Conn, Joseph L. "Storm Clouds Over the Sunshine State." Americans United for Church and State. June 2008. https://www.au.org/church-state/june-2008-church-state/featured/storm-clouds-over-the-sunshine-state.

Costello-Dougherty, Malaika. "Waldorf-Inspired Public Schools Are on the Rise." *Edutopia*, August 31, 2009. http://www.edutopia.org/waldorf-public-school-morse.

CREDO. Center for Research on Education Outcomes. "Charter Schools Make Gains, According to 26-State Study." 2013. credo.stanford.edu/documents/UNEMBARGOED%20National%20Charter%20Study%20Press%20Release.pdf.

Minneapolis Public Schools. Licensing Program Information. CUE Programs. Humanresources.mpls.k12.mn.us/licensing_programs.

Darling-Hammond, Linda, Deborah J. Holtzman, Su Jin Gatlin, and Julian Vasquez Heilig. "Does Teacher Preparation Matter? Evidence about Teacher Certification, Teach for America, and Teacher Effectiveness." *Education Policy Analysis Archives* 13, no. 42 (2005): 1–47.

Decker, Paul T., Daniel P. Mayor, and Steven Glazerman. "The Effects of Teach for America on Students: Findings from a National Evaluation." Mathematica Policy Research, Inc. June 9, 2004. http://www.mathematica-mpr.com/publications/pdfs/teach.pdf.

Department of Law & Public Safety. "Head of Private Education Services Corporation Sentenced to Prison for Fraudulently Overbilling Districts 1.3 Million." Office of the Attorney General. October 3, 2008. http://www.nj.gov/oag/newsreleases08/pr20081003a.html.

deVise, Daniel. "Bill Gates Talks about Teacher Pay, Class Size." *Washington Post*, February 28, 2011.

Dillon, Sam. "2 School Entrepreneurs Lead the Way on Change." *New York Times*, June 19, 2008.

Dixon, Felicia. "Differentiating Instruction in AP: An Important Question? Or, Out of the Question?" *Gifted Child Today* 29, no. 2 (2006): 50–54.

Dixon, Jennifer. "Michigan Spends $1 Billion on Charter Schools But Fails to Hold Them Accountable." *Detroit Free Press*, June 22, 2014.

Donald R. McAdams, PhD. Reasoning Minds. http://www.reasoningmind.org/biography/donald-mcadams/.

Doyle, Rodger. "Sizing Up Evangelicals." *Scientific American* 288, no. 3 (2003): 37.

Dreilinger, Danielle. "Landmark New Orleans Special Education Case Is Settled, Parties Say." *Times-Picayune*, December 19, 2014.

Dudley, Anne, and Ellis and Kerri Ginis. "Fresno Charter School in Furor: Unusual Punishments, Testing Violations Alleged as Principal Resigns." *Fresno Bee*, February 20, 2009. http://susanohanian.org/show_atrocities.php?id=8427.

EdisonLearning. http://edisonlearning.com/.

Editorial. "An American Family." *Wall Street Journal*, July 8, 2005.

Eli and Edythe Broad. The Broad Foundation. http://broadfoundation.org/about_broads.html.

Emery, Kathy. "The Business Roundtable and Systemic Reform: How Corporate-Engineered High-Stakes Testing Has Eliminated Community Participation in Developing Educational Goals and Policies." Dissertation. University of California Davis, 2002.

Emery, Kathy, and Susan Ohanian. *Why Is Corporate America Bashing Our Public Schools?* Portsmouth, NH: Heinemann, 2004, 141–64.

*e School News*. "Grants to Bennett's K12 Inc. Challenged." August 16, 2004. http://www.eschoolnews.com/news/top-news/index.cfm?i=35921&page=2.

Family Educational Rights and Privacy Act (FERPA). US Department of Education. 20 USC. § 1232g; 34 CFR Part 99. http://www.ed.gov/policy/gen/guid/fpco/ferpa/index.html.

Fang, Lee. "Ted Mitchell, Education Dept. Nominee, Has Strong Ties to Pearson Privatization Movement." *The Nation*, December 19, 2013. http://www.thenation.com/blog/177675/ted-mitchell-education-dept-nominee-has-strong-ties-pearson-privatization-movement#.

Feng, Betty, and Jeff Krehely. "The Waltons and Wal-Mart Self-Interested Philanthropy." National Committee for Responsive Philanthropy, September 2005. http://reclaimdemocracy.org/wordpress/wp-content/uploads/2012/08/walton_philanthropy.pdf.

Finn, Chester E., and Kathleen Madigan. "Removing the Barriers for Teacher Candidates." *Educational Leadership* 58, no. 8 (2001): 29–36.

Fischer, Kent. "Public School Inc." *St. Petersburg Times*, September 15, 2002.

Florida Department of Education. School Choice. http://www.fldoe.org/schools/school-choice/.

Foundation for Excellence in Education. http://excelined.org/.

Fratt, Lisa. "Edison Buyout Draws Ire in Florida." *District Administration*. February Update, 2004. http://www.districtadministration.com/viewarticle.aspx?articleid=472.

Friedman Foundation for Educational Choice. "What Is School Choice?" http://www.edchoice.org/School-Choice/What-is-School-Choice.aspx.

Futurist Speaker Thomas Frey. "Teacherless Education and the Competition That Will Change Everything." www.futuristspeaker.com/2012/04/teacherless-education-and-the-competition-that-will-change-everything/.

Garcia-Roberts, Gus. "McKay Scholarship Program Sparks a Cottage Industry of Fraud and Chaos." *Miami New Times*, June 23, 2011.

Gates, Bill. "Bill Gates: Commend Common Core." *USA Today*, February 12, 2014.

Gerstner, Louis V., Jr., Roger D. Semerad, Denis Philip Doyle, and William B. Johnston. *Reinventing Education: Entrepreneurship in America's Public Schools*. New York: Penguin Books, 1995, 78–79, 25–30, 35–41.

Gewertz, Catherine. "Acquisition News in the World of Common Standards, Tests." Curriculum Matters. *Education Week*, August 4, 2010. http://blogs.edweek.org/edweek/curriculum/2010/08/acquisition_news_in_the_world.html.

Gillum, Jack and Marisol Bello. "When Standardized Test Scores Soared in D.C., Were the Gains Real?" *USA Today*. March 30, 2011.

Glass, Gene V., and Kevin G. Welner. "Online K–12 Schooling in the US: Uncertain Private Ventures in Need of Public Regulation." Boulder, CO: National Education Policy Center, October 2011. http://nepc.colorado.edu/files/NEPC-VirtSchool-1-PB-Glass-Welner.pdf.

Goodgame, Dan. "Calling for an Overhaul." *TIME*, October 9, 1989.

Gordon, Howard R. D. *The History and Growth of Vocational Education in America*, 3rd ed. Prospect Heights, IL: Waveland Press Inc., 2008, 94.

Grannan, Caroline. "14 of 15 Green Dot Schools Are 'Failing,' by Parent Revolution's Definition." *San Francisco Examiner*, January 14, 2010.

Green, Elizabeth. "Jon Schnur, 'Ideolocrat' Poster Boy Will Not Work for Obama." Chalkbeat New York. May 1, 2009.

Green, Jay, and William C. Symonds. "Bill Gates Gets Schooled." *Business Week*, June 26, 2006.

Haimson, Leonie. "It's Apparently the End of the Line for inBloom, But Not Our Fight to Protect Student Privacy." Class Size Matters, April 2, 2014. http://www.classsizematters.org/its-apparently-the-end-of-the-line-for-inbloom-but-not-our-fight-to-protect-student-privacy/.

Harris, Alisa. "Getting Religion." *World* 24, no. 23 (2009). http://www.worldmag.com/articles/16090.

Harris, Debbi, and David N. Plank. "Who's Teaching in Michigan's Traditional and Charter Public Schools?" The Educational Policy Center at Michigan State University. Policy Report No. 17. May 2003. http://education.msu.edu/epc/forms/policy-and-research-reports/report17.pdf.

Harris, Elizabeth A. "20% of New York State Students Opted Out of Standardized Tests This Year." *New York Times*, August 12, 2015.

Helfand, Duke, and Peter Nicholas. "Wanted: Schools Chief with Zero Experience." *Los Angeles Times*, April 20, 2005.

Henig, Jerry R. *Spin Cycle: How Research Gets Used in Policy Debates: The Case of Charter Schools.* New York: Russell Sage Foundation Publications, 2008, 3.

Herrera, Laura. "In Florida, Virtual Classrooms with No Teachers." *New York Times*, January 17, 2011.

Hing, Julianne. "College Students Wage Campaign to Kick Teach for America Off of Campus." Colorlines News for Action, September 30, 2014. http://colorlines.com/archives/2014/09/college_students_wage_campaign_to_kick_teach_for_america_off_of_campus.html.

Honawar, Vaishali. "Suit Contests 'Loophole' for Alternate Paths." *Education Week* 27, no. 1 (2007): 24.

Hood, Grace. "K12 Inc.: Public Online Schools, Private Profits." Community Radio for Northern Colorado. NPR, September 21, 2011. http://kunc.org/post/k12-inc-public-online-schools-private-profits.

Hopkins, Jim. "Wal-Mart Heirs Pour Riches into Education Reform." *USA Today*, March 11, 2004.

Horn, James. "KIPP Forces 5th Graders to 'Earn' Desks by Sitting on the Floor for a Week." AlterNet, December 17, 2013. http://www.alternet.org/education/kipp-forces-5th-graders-earn-desks-sitting-floor-week?page=0%2C1.

Horn, Jim. "Feds Continue to Shovel Money to Charter Scams and Encourage High Poverty Quotas." Schools Matter, January 10, 2012. http://www.schoolsmatter.info/2012/01/feds-continue-to-shovel-money-to.html.

———. "Kevin Huffman Huffs and Puffs: Nashville School Board Stands Strong." Schools Matter, September 18, 2012. http://www.schoolsmatter.info/2012/09/kevin-huffman-huffs-and-puffs-nashville.html.

Horowitz, Evan. "What Happens to Students Who Fail the PARCC Exam?" *Boston Globe*, March 18, 2015.

Hu, Winnie. "Seeing No Progress, Some Schools Drop Laptops." *New York Times*, May 4, 2007.

Illinois Online Network. Weaknesses of Online Learning. http://www.ion.uillinois.edu/resources/tutorials/overview/weaknesses.asp.

InBloom. 2014. https://www.inbloom.org/about-inbloom.

International Baccalaureate Organization. Support for Implementation Services. http://www.ibo.org/become/fees/applicationfees/.

Jacobson, Susan. "Florida Virtual School Sues Own Foundation." *Orlando Sentinel*, May 8, 2015.

Johnson, Dale D., Bonnie Johnson, Stephen J. Farenga, and Daniel Ness. *Trivalizing Teacher Education: The Accreditation Squeeze.* Lanham, Maryland: Rowman & Littlefield Publishers, 2005, 73.

Josephson, Michael S. "Implementation of President Bush's Campaign Commitments Concerning Character Education." White Paper to the President's Transition Team on Education, December 23, 2000. http://charactercounts.org/WhPaper12-23-00.htm.

Josephson, Michael S. "OBSERVATION: President Barack Obama on CHARACTER COUNTS! Week." What Will Matter, October 23, 2012. http://whatwillmatter.com/2012/10/observation-president-barack-obama-on-character-counts-week/.

K12. How a K12 Education Works. http://www.k12.com/what-is-k12/how-k12-programs-work/.

Kaestle, Carl F. "Part One: 1770–1900—The Common School: The Educated Citizen." In *School: The Story of American Public Education*, ed. Sarah Mondale and Sarah B. Patton. Boston: Beacon Press, 2001, 33–38.

Kahlenberg, Richard D. *Tough Liberal: Albert Shanker and the Battles Over Schools, Unions, Race, and Democracy*. New York: Columbia University Press, 2007, 313–14.

Kelly, William J. "The Next 50 Chicago Public Schools Rahm Emanuel Will Close." Kelly Truth Squad, February 23, 2015.

"KIPP: Are We Building a Sustainable Financial Model?" 2014 Report Card. http://www.kipp.org/question6.

Kleinknecht, William. *The Man Who Sold the World: Ronald Reagan and the Betrayal of Main Street America*. New York: Nation Books, 2009, 6.

Konnikova, Maria. "Will MOOCS Be Flukes?" *The New Yorker*, November 7, 2014.

Kovacs, Philip. "Gates, Buffet, and the Corporatization of Children." Common Dreams, June 28, 2006. www.commondreams.org/views/2006/06/28/gates-buffett-and-corporatization-children.

Kugler, John. "Rhee Bragged About Taping Students' Mouths Shut While She Was a Teach for America 'Teacher.'" *Substance News*, September 22, 2010.

Labbe, Theola. "New Schools Chief Builds Team." *Washington Post*, June 23, 2007.

LaCoste-Caputo, Jenny. "They Aren't Going to Take It Anymore." *San Antonio Express-News*, February 19, 2005.

Lafer, Gordon. "Do Poor Kids Deserve Lower-Quality Education Than Rich Kids? Evaluating School Privatization Proposals in Milwaukee Wisconsin." Economic Policy Institute, April 24, 2013. http://www.epi.org/publication/school-privatization-milwaukee/.

Layton, Lyndsey. "How Bill Gates Pulled Off the Swift Common Core Revolution." *Washington Post*, June 7, 2014.

Layton, Lyndsey, and Emma Brown. "Virtual Schools Are Multiplying, but Some Question Their Educational Value." *Washington Post*, November 26, 2011.

The League of Women Voters of Florida. Final Report. Statewide Study on School Choice and Consensus Report on Charter Schools. Florida League of Women Voters Education Team. April 20, 2014.

Leaming, Jeremy. "Charter for Controversy." Americans United for Separation of Church and State, June 2003. http://www.au.org/site/News2?news_iv_ctrl=-1&abbr=cs_&page=NewsArticle&id=5359.

Leave My Child Alone! Opt Out of the Pentagon's Database and Your School's Military Recruitment List. High School Opt Out. http://themmob.org/lmca/optout.html.

Lier, Piet van. "Analyzing Autism Vouchers in Ohio." A Report from Policy Matters Ohio, March 2008. www.policymattersohio.org/wp-content/uploads/2011/09/AnalyzingAutismVouchers2008_0319.pdf.

Lopez, Shane J. "Parents, Americans Much More Positive About Local Schools." Gallup, August 19, 2011. http://www.gallup.com/poll/149093/parents-americans-positive-local-schools.aspx.

Magan, Christopher. "In Minnesota, Teach for America Offers New Way to Be Classroom Instructor." *Pioneer Press*, August 22, 2015.

Magaziner, Ira C., and Hillary Rodham Clinton. "Will America Choose High Skills or Low Wages?" *Educational Leadership* 49, no. 6 (1992): 10–14.

Manzo, Kathleen Kennedy. "Fla. Budget Threatens Online Ed Mandate." *Education Week* 28, no. 30 (2009): 1, 12–13.

Marr, Kendra. "States Opt Out of School Funding." POLITICO 44, June 1, 2010. http://www.politico.com/politico44/perm/0610/race_to_the_top_c7a6aaba-8c09-491a-a5bc-c1c57f484b2b.html.

Martin, Doug. *Hoosier School Heist.* Indianapolis: Brooks Publications, 2014, 106–9, 46.

Matheson, Kathy. "Microsoft 'School of the Future' in Philly Finally in a Groove?" *USA Today*, June 19, 2010.

Mathis, William J., and Gary Miron. "Report Shows Students Attending K12 Inc. Cyber Schools Fall Behind." National Education Policy Center, July 18, 2012. http://nepc.colorado.edu/newsletter/2012/07/understanding-improving-virtual.

McClure, Vicki, and Mary Shanklin. "Cashing in on Kids." *Orlando Sentinel*, March 27, 2007.

McGrory, Kathleen. "Bill Would Allow Online Vendors Better Access to Public School Funding." *Miami Herald*, May 10, 2013.

McGrory, Kathleen, and Jeffrey S. Solocheck. "Teachers Challenge Testing for Special-Needs Students." *Miami Herald*, February 26, 2014.

McLeod, Saul A. "Kohlberg." Simply Psychology, 2011. http://www.simplypsychology.org/kohlberg.html.

Mencimer, Stephanie. "Jeb Bush's Cyber Attack on Public Schools." *Mother Jones* , November/December 2011.

*Meredith v. Jefferson County Board of Education*, 126 S.Ct 2738 (2007).

Merrow, John. "Michelle Rhee's Reign of Error." Taking Note, April 11, 2013. http://takingnote.learningmatters.tv/?p=6232.

Micucci, Jackie. "How Garfield High Defeated the MAP Test." *Seattle*, August 2013.

Miller, Kimberly, and Shirish Date. "Voucher Bargain May Cost Taxpayers." *Palm Beach Post*, September 20, 2003.

Mills, Mike. "Michelle Rhee Reveals Her Plans for the Private Sector's Role in D.C. School Reform." *Washington Business Journal*, April 28, 2008. http://www.bizjournals.com/washington/stories/2008/04/28/story2.html?page=all.

Milner, Richard H. IV. "Review of 'Teacher Evaluation 2.0.'" National Education Policy Center. http://nepc.colorado.edu/files/TTR-TeachEval2.0-Milner-FINAL.pdf.

Miner, Barbara. "Looking Past the Spin." *Rethinking Schools* 24, no. 3 (2010): 24–33.

Miron, Gary, and Jessica L. Urschel. "A Study of Student Characteristics, School Finance, and School Performance in Schools Operated by K12 Inc." Boulder, CO: National Education Policy Center. July 2012. http://nepc.colorado.edu/publication/understanding-improving-virtual.

Miron, Gary, Jessica Urschel, William J. Mathis, and Elana Tornquist. "Schools without Diversity: Education Management Organizations, Charter Schools, and the Demographic Stratification of the American School System." NEPC, February 5, 2010.

Miron, Gary, Jessica L. Urschel, and Nicholas Saxton. "What Makes KIPP Work? A Study of Student Characteristics Attrition, and School Finance." College of Education and Human Development Western Michigan University, March 2011. http://www.edweek.org/media/kippstudy.pdf.

Mishel, Lawrence, and Joydeep Roy. "Where Our High-School Dropout Crisis Really Is." *Education Digest* 72, no. 6 (2007): 12–21.

Mitchell, Nancy, and Burt Hubbard. "Test Scores Raise Questions About Colo. Virtual Schools." *Education Week* 31, no. 6 (2011): 10.

Moberg, David. "How Edison Survived: Discredited and Broke, the School Privatizer Found an Unlikely White Knight." *The Nation*, March 15, 2004.

Monahan, Rachel, and Ben Chapman. "Padded 'Calm-Down' Room at Charter School Drives Kids to Anxiety Attacks." *New York Daily News*, December 11, 2013.

National Center for Education Statistics. Program for International Student Assessment. Institute of Education Sciences. nces.ed.gov/surveys/pisa/.

National Coalition to Protect Student Privacy. "The ASVAB Campaign." http://www.studentprivacy.org/asvab-campaign.html.

National Council on Teacher Quality (NCTQ). About NCTQ. http://www.nctq.org/about/advisoryBoard.jsp.

———. "Attracting, Developing and Retaining US Department of Education: Background Report for the United States." International Affairs Office, October 2004. http://www.nctq.org/dmsView/Attracting_Developing_and_Retaining_Effective_Teachers_NCTQ_USDE_Report.

National Heritage Academies. http://heritageacademies.com/about-us/our_story/.

"A Nation Prepared: Teachers for the 21st Century. The Report of the Task Force on Teaching as a Profession." ERIC ED 268120. New York: Carnegie Corporation, 168. 1986.

The Nation's Report Card, 2013. http://nationsreportcard.gov/reading_math_2013/#/performance-overview.

Neufeld, Sara. "Pa. Firm to Run Special-Education School." *Baltimore Sun*, May 29, 2008.

"New Leaders for New Schools." Center for American Progress. March 10, 2008. www.americanprogress.org/events/2008/03/10/16612/new-leaders-for-new-schools/.

NewSchools Venture Fund. http://newschools.org/.

The New Teacher Project. Our People. tntp.org/about-tntp/our-people.

No Child Left Behind. Charter Schools Program. Title V, Part B. Non-Regulatory Guidance. Department of Education. July 2004.

Noguchi, Sharon. "Rocketship Education Changes Course, Slows Expansion." *San Jose Mercury News*, June 28, 2014.

NYC Schools: Expect Turbulence Ahead." *New York Daily News*, November 9, 2010.

O'Brien, Erin. "'America 2000' Sets 6 Goals for Improving Education Nationwide." *Sun Sentinel*, February 26, 1992.

O'Connor, John. "Georgia Threatens to Close K12-run Online Charter School." State Impact. November 26, 2012. Stateimpact.npr.org/florida/2012/11/26/georgia-threatens-to-close-k12-run-online-charter-school/.

Ollstein, Alice. "This City Is Fighting Against Public School Privatization." Think Progress, June 14, 2015.

"Online Charter School Students Falling Behind Their Peers." Mathematica Policy Research, Center on Reinventing Public Eduation, and Center for Research on Education Outcomes. October 27, 2015.

Oppenheimer, Todd. "Computer Illogic/Despite Great Promise, Technology Is Dumbing Down the Classroom." San Francisco Gate, November 30, 2003. http://articles.sfgate.com/2003-11-30/opinion/17518775_1_school-libraries-classroom-computers-education-policy.

Organization for Economic Cooperation and Development (OECD). "Students, Computers and Learning: Making the Connection." Programme for International Student Assessment, October 2015. http://www.keepeek.com/Digital-Asset-Management/oecd/education/students-computers-and-learning_9789264239555-en#page2.

Overview of the SchoolWorks Quality. Criteria 3rd Edition. Developed for the 2008 Broad Prize for Urban Education. www.broadprize.org/asset/1100-tbpschoolworksqualitycriteria.pdf.

Pan, Deanna. "14 Wacky 'Facts' Kids Will Learn in Louisiana's Voucher Schools." *Mother Jones*, April 7, 2012. www.motherjones.com/blue-marble/2012/07/photos-evangelical-curricula-louisiana-tax-dollars.

*Parents Involved in Community Schools v. Seattle School District No. 1*, 551 US 701 (2007).

Pennington, Kaitlen. "The Nation's Largest Teachers Union Calls for Revamp of Teacher—Pay System." Center for American Progress, October 25, 2013. http://www.americanprogress.org/issues/education/news/2013/10/25/77986/the-nations-largest-teachers-union-calls-for-revamp-of-teacher-pay-system/.

Perez, Juan Jr. "Dyett High School Hunger Strike Ends." *Chicago Tribune*, September 20, 2015.

Pogash, Carol. "Public Financing Supports Growth of Online Charter Schools." *The New York Times*. June 4, 2010.

Pullman, Joy. "Data Mining Kids Crosses Line." Heartline, March 16, 2013. http://news.heartland.org/editorial/2013/03/16/data-mining-kids-crosses-line.

Ravitch, Diane. *The Death and Life of the Great American School System*. New York: Basic Books, 2007, 203.

———. "Is the Charter Movement Imploding?" Diane Ravitch's blog, July 5, 2014.

———. *Reign of Error: The Hoax of the Privatization Movement and the Danger to America's Public Schools*. New York: Alfred A. Knopf, 2013, 210.

Reckdahl, Katy. "Parents, Advocates Fear That New Orleans Charter Schools Have Rejected Students with Disabilities." *Times-Picayune*, June 5, 2010.

Relay Graduate School Education. About. http://www.relay.edu/about/partners.

Richards, Erin, and Patrick Simonaitis. "Most Students Applying for State Voucher Program Attend Private Schools." *Journal Sentinel*, August 15, 2013.

Richtel, Matt. "In Classroom of Future, Stagnant Scores." *New York Times*, September 3, 2011.

Ritchie, Susan. "Horace Mann." Unitarian Universalist History and Heritage Society. 1999–2013.http://www25.uua.org/uuhs/duub/articles/horacemann.html.

Roberts, Jane. "Schools to Pen Pact for $3.2M." *Commercial Appeal*, October 17, 2009.

Robinson, B. A. "A 'Moment of Silence' in Place of Prayer in US Public Schools." http://www.religioustolerance.org/ps_pra6.htm.

Rockwell, Lilly. "Jonathan Hage." Florida Trend, December 26, 2012. http://www.floridatrend.com/article/15060/jonathan-hage.

Rose, Charlie. "The Giving Pledge: A New Club for Billionaires." CBS *60 Minutes*, November 17, 2013. http://www.cbsnews.com/news/the-giving-pledge-a-new-club-for-billionaires/.

Rosenblith, Suzanne, and Bea Bailey. "Comprehensive Religious Studies in Public Education: Educating for a Religiously Literate Society." *Educational Studies (American Educational Studies Association)* 42, no. 2 (2007): 93–111.

Rothstein, Jesse, and William J. Mathis. "Review of Two Culminating Projects from the MET Project." National Education Policy Center, January 2013. http://nepc.colorado.edu/thinktank/review-MET-final-2013.

Russ, Valerie. "School of the Future Having Problems in the Present." *Philadelphia Daily News*, May 27, 2010.

Ryman, Anne and Pat Kossan. "Cheating by Online Students a Concern." The Arizona Republic. December 12, 2011. www.azcentral.com/news/articles/2011/12/12/20111212cheating-by-online-students-concern.html.

Safier, David. "An Explanation of the AZVA Outsourcing Process." Blog for Arizona, 2008. http://arizona.typepad.com/blog/2008/08/an-explanation.html.

*Santa Fe Independent School District v. Doe*, 530 US 290 (2000).

Saul, Stephanie. "Profits and Questions at Online Charter Schools." *New York Times*, December 12, 2011.

Sawchuk, Stephen. "N.C. District Lets Go of Veteran Teachers, But Keeps TFA Hires." *Education Week* 28, no. 35 (2009): 10.

———. "Tenn. Teachers' Union Takes Evaluation Fight into the Courtroom." *Education Week* 33, no. 27 (2014): 8–9.

Schaffer, Bob, Hon. of Colorado. "Dollars to the Classroom Act." Speech presented in the House of Representatives, September 17, 1998.

Schemo, Diana Jean. "Charter Schools Trail in Results, US Data Reveals." *New York Times*, August 17, 2004.

Schemo, Diana Jean. "Education Secretary Defends Charter Schools." *New York Times* Education, August 18, 2004.

Schneider, John. "Military Recruiters Have Eye on Students." *Baltimore Sun*, December 22, 2005.

Schneider, Mercedes. "Those 24 Common Core 2009 Work Group Members." deutsch29, April 23, 2014. http://deutsch29.wordpress.com/2014/04/23/those-24-common-core-2009-work-group-members/.

*School Choice Ohio. EdChoice Scholarship Program.* http://www.scohio.org/school-options/choose-school-options/private-school/ohioscholarships/edchoice.html.

Scott, Janelle. 2009. "The Politics of Venture Philanthropy in Charter School Policy and Advocacy." *Educational Policy* 23, no. 1 (2009): 106–36.

Shieh, David. "Professors Regard Online Instruction as Less Effective Than Classroom Learning." *Chronicle of Higher Education*, February 10, 2009.

Shierholz, Heidi, Alyssa Davis, and Will Kimball. "The Class of 2014: The Weak Economy Is Idling Too Many Young Graduates." Economic Policy Institute, May 1, 2014. http://www.epi.org/publication/class-of-2014/.

Skeels, Robert D. "Political Patronage for Green Dot Public Schools' Chief Propagandist." The Daily Censored, April 24, 2010. http://www.dailycensored.com/political-patronage-for-green-dot-public-schools-chief-propagandist/.

Smith, Doug, and Max Brantley. "Conservative Think-Tanker to Head UA School-Reform Operation." *Arkansas Times*, July 28, 2005.

Social and Character Development Research Consortium. Efficacy of Schoolwide Programs to Promote Social and Character Development and Reduce Problem Behavior in Elementary School Children (NCER 2011–2001). Washington, DC: National Center for Education Research, Institute of Education Sciences, US Department of Education, 2010.

*Social Enterprise*. "Harvard Alumni Preparing Leaders for Urban Schools." Harvard Business School, Spring 2001. www.hbs.edu/socialenterprise/Pages/default.aspx.

Solnet, Rita M. "Florida Vouchers: This Is Choice?" Huffington Post, May 18, 2014, http://www.huffingtonpost.com/rita-m-solnet/florida-vouchers-this-is-_b_4980612.html.

Sourcewatch: The Center for Media and Democracy. "Connections Academy." http://www.sourcewatch.org/index.php/Connections_Academy.

Southern Poverty Law Center. "Judge Denies Motion to Dismiss SPLC Suit Seeking Equal Education for Special Needs Students in New Orleans." April 25, 2011. http://www.splcenter.org/get-informed/news/judge-denies-motion-to-dismiss-splc-suit-seeking-equal-education-for-special-needs-students.

Specialized Education Services, Inc. http://www.sesi-schools.com/.

Stansbury, Meris. "School of the Future: Lessons in Failure." *eSchool News*, June 1, 2009. http://www.eschoolnews.com/2009/06/01/school-of-the-future-lessons-in-failure/.

Stein, Jason. "Lobbyists Keep Working Despite Convictions." *Journal Sentinel*, June 19, 2010.

Stephens, Scott. "Charters Use Teachers Not Fully Certified: Traditional Schools Held to Higher Standards When Picking Instructors." *The Plain Dealer*, February 24, 2005.

Stewart, Katherine. "Reading, Writing, and Original Sin." *Santa Barbara Independent*, May 7, 2009.

Stop Rocketship Now! http://www.stoprocketship.com/.

"Stratification of the American School System." Boulder and Tempe: Education and Public Interest Center & Education Policy Research Unit, February 2010.

Sullivan, Maureen. "Liberals Fight to Keep Students Locked in Nevada's Failing Public Schools." *Forbes*, August 30, 2015.

Swanson, Carl. "How Do You Say 'Early Admission' in Mandarin?" *New York Magazine*, September 9, 2012. http://nymag.com/print/?/news/features/avenues-school-chris-whittle-2012-9/.

Tabachnick, Rachel. "The Religious Right's Plot to Take Control of Our Public Schools." AlterNet, March 6, 2012. http://www.alternet.org/visions/154435/the_religious_right%27s_plot_to_take_control_of_our_public_schools.

Teach for America. Americorps Benefits. https://www.teachforamerica.org/why-teach-for-america/compensation-and-benefits/assistance-pre-existing-loans.

———. Donors. http://www.teachforamerica.org/about/our_donors.htm.

Thomas B. Fordham Foundation. Five-Year Report. 1997–2001. May 2002.

Tilove, Jonathan. "Can a Young Korean-American Woman Save D.C.'s Schools?" *Newhouse News Service*, 2007.

Toch, Thomas. "America's Choice School Design." *School Administrator*, January 2005. http://www.aasa.org/SchoolAdministratorArticle.aspx?id=8852.

Toppo, Greg, and Dan Vergano. "Scientist Shortage? Maybe Not." *USA Today*, July 9, 2009.

The Tripod Project. Cambridge Education. http://tripodproject.org/contact-us-to-plan-your-survey/.

Trotter, Andrew. "Disruptive Innovation." *Education Week's Digital Directions*, Fall 2008.

———. "K12 Inc. Scraps India Outsourcing." *Education Week* 28, no. 3 (2008): 1, 14–15.

Trucano, Michael. "Worst Practice in ICT Use in Education." *EduTech*, April 30, 2010. http://blogs.worldbank.org/edutech/worst-practice.

Truth About IB. Fees. http://truthaboutib.com/howmuchdoesibcost/ibfees.html.

Tucker, Jill. "Teachers' Dim Future: Budget Cuts, Cramped Classes." *San Francisco Chronicle*, December 14, 2010.

Turner, Jim. "Florida Virtual School v. K12 Inc.: Supreme Court Clears Way for Legal Fight." FlaglerLive.com, September 18, 2014. http://flaglerlive.com/70507/flvs-k12inc/.

Underwood, Julie. "Starving Public Schools." *The Nation* 293, no. 5&6 (2011): 21–23.

United Opt Out. http://unitedoptout.com/.

United States Charter Schools. Contracts with Parents and Students. http://www.uscharterschools.org/cs/r/view/uscs_rs/472.

US Department of Education. Green Dot Charter Schools. http://www.ed.gov/labor-management-collaboration/conference/green-dot-public-schools.

———. James H. Shelton, III. Assistant Deputy Secretary for Innovation and Improvement—Biography. http://www2.ed.gov/news/staff/bios/shelton.html.

———. Senior Staff. Margot Rogers. Chief of Staff—Biography. http://www2.ed.gov/news/staff/bios/mrogers.html.

———. States Impact on Federal Education Policy. NY State Archives. Federal Education Policy and the States, 1945–2009. The George H. W. Bush Years: America 2000 Proposed. nysa32.nysed.gov/edpolicy/research/res_essay_bush_ghw_edsummit.shtml.

———. Thelma Melendez de Santa Ana, Assistant Secretary for Elementary and Secondary—Biography. http://www2.ed.gov/news/staff/bios/melendez.html.

US Department of Labor. Bureau of Labor Statistics. Economic News Release. Table 7. The 30 Occupations with the Fastest Projected Employment Growth, 2010–2020 (In Thousands). http://www.bls.gov/news.release/ecopro.t07.htm.

Vail, Kathleen. "A Changing World." *American School Board Journal* 194, no. 2 (2007): 14–19.

Van Roekel, Dennis. "We Need a Course Correction on Common Core." *NEA Today*, February 19, 2014. http://neatoday.org/2014/02/19/nea-president-we-need-a-course-correction-on-common-core/.

*Vergara v. State of California*, 2014.

Viadero, Debra. "Teaching to the Test." *Education Week*, July 13, 1994.

Vogell, Heather. "Charter School Faces Withdrawals over Punishment." *Atlanta Journal Constitution*, March 22, 2009. http://charterschoolscandals.blogspot.com/2010/05/kipp-south-fulton-academy.html.

Wallis, Claudia. "The Evolution Wars." *Time* 166, no. 7 (2005): 26–35.

Walsh, Joan. "The Shame of San Francisco." *Salon*, March 29, 2001. http://www.salon.com/2001/03/29/edison/.

Walsh, Mark. 2001. "Former Education Secretary Starts Online-Learning Venture." *Education Week* 20, no. 16 (2001): 7.

Weisberg, Daniel, Susan Sexton, Jennifer Mulhern, and David Keeling. "The Widget Effect: Our National Failure to Acknowledge and Act on Differences in Teacher Effectiveness." The New Teacher Project, 2009. http://widgeteffect.org/downloads/TheWidgetEffect.pdf.

Wolf, Susan, and Mira Browne. "New Stanford Report Finds Serious Quality Challenge in National Charter School Sector." Press Release, June 15, 2009. http://credo.stanford.edu/reports/National_Release.pdf.

Worthen, Maria and Lillian Pace. "A K-12 Federal Policy Framework for Competency Education: Building Capacity for Systems Change." Competency Works Issue Brief. February 2014.

Wyatt, Edward. "Charter School to Raise Topic of Creationism." *New York Times*, February 18, 2000.

Yao, Deborah. "Microsoft-Designed School Opens in Pa." *Boston Globe*, September 7, 2006.

Zirkel, Perry A. "Parent/Student Religious Activities. *Principal* 87, no. 3 (2008): 8–10.

# Index

# About the Author

**Nancy E. Bailey**, PhD, taught students with a wide range of beautiful differences in special education for many years. She is the author of *Misguided Education Reform: Debating the Impact on Students*. Bailey can be found advocating for democratic public schools on her blog, Nancy Bailey's Education Website, at www.nancyebailey.com.